THE
PRESIDENTIAL
NOMINATING PROCESS

Constitutional, Economic
and Political Issues

The George Gund Lectures
Volume III

Edited by

Kenneth W. Thompson

Director
The White Burkett Miller Center of Public Affairs
University of Virginia

UNIVERSITY
PRESS OF
AMERICA

LANHAM • NEW YORK • LONDON

Library of Congress Cataloging in Publication Data
(Revised for volume 3)

Main entry under title:

The Presidential nominating process.

Lectures organized by the White Burkett Miller
Center of Public Affairs.
1. Presidents—United States—Nomination—
Addresses, essays, lectures. I. Thompson, Kenneth W.,
1921-   . II. White Burkett Miller Center.

JK521.P733   1983   324.5'0973   83-6790
ISBN 0-8191-4151-8 (v. 3)
ISBN 0-8191-4152-6 (pbk.: v. 3)

Dedicated

to

Paul and Opal David
Pioneer scholar and path breaking political leader
who in their lives and work
have thrown a clear light
on aspects of
the nominating and electoral process

Table of Contents

PREFACE

Beginning in 1981, the Council and staff of the Miller Center began a review of the most urgent issues confronting the nation and the presidency with the aim of establishing program priorities. One issue that rose to the surface in every exchange was that of the relation of the presidency and the press and the media. Responding to the unquestioned importance of the problem, a national commission co-chaired by Governor Linwood Holton and Ray Scherer, Vice President of RCA, was formed. Its report inspired the reorganization of presidential press conferences by the Reagan administration. Complementing the Commission's Report, six monographic volumes were published as part of the Center's efforts in this area with titles as wide-ranging as *Ten Presidents and the Press; The White House Press on the Presidency; Presidents, Prime Ministers, and the Press;* and *Three Press Secretaries on the Presidency and the Press.*

Following the pattern established in the study of the presidency and the media, a second national commission was established, this one to review the large issue of the presidential nominating process. The new commission was chaired by Melvin R. Laird and Adlai E. Stevenson III with Governor Holton as Executive Board Chairman. It carried forward its work through the efforts of an executive board of ten members and a larger group of forty governors. As with the study of the press, commission deliberations were combined with the preparation of scholarly papers and the presentation of the George Gund Lectures. The present volume is the third in a series of volumes bringing together the lectures and papers.

A third urgent issue to which the Center is directing attention is that of presidential transitions and foreign policy. Former secretaries of state William P. Rogers and Cyrus Vance chair the third Miller Center commission on this subject with members including Dean Rusk, Harold Brown, Walter Cronkite, Clark Clifford, General Andrew Goodpaster, Carol Laise, Jane Cahill Pfeiffer, and Theodore Sorensen. The staff director of the commission is Frederick Mosher who is writing a book on the subject. Lectures, conferences and carefully researched case studies are being organized to reenforce the commission's efforts.

The Miller Center and its staff consider that the approach it is employing in the work of the three commissions and the related scholarly research and writing has marked out a new and promising method for the study of urgent problems. It intends to follow this approach in such future inquires as may be directed by its Council.

INTRODUCTION

Each volume in the George Gund Lecture series is addressed to a separate cluster of issues and concerns relating to the presidential nominating process. Volume I provided an introduction to the subject with emphasis on the theory, history, practice and controversies surrounding the process. Volume II sought both to broaden and narrow the debate. It examined broad proposals for constitutional reform reaching substantially beyond the nominating process as such. Other contributors questioned whether either constitutional or political and procedural changes were needed. These observers sought to narrow the question to issues involving personality characteristics of the candidates. Thus Volume II constituted approaches that widened and narrowed the scope of discussion on the nominating process.

The third volume focuses on constitutional, economic and political issues. Chancellor Emeritus Alexander Heard of Vanderbilt University sets forth the constitutional basis for analyzing the selection process. Having resumed his work as Professor of Political Science and taken on the responsibility of director of a long-term study of the "presidential selection process" with support of the Alfred P. Sloan Foundation, Chancellor Heard kindly shared some of his preliminary reflections and findings with a large audience of faculty, students and community leaders in the Dome Room of the Rotunda. It may be significant that his is the first lecture in the series to emphasize constitutional issues.

Professor David Price of Duke University, executive director of the Hunt Commission study, and Albert Beveridge III of the Federal Election Commission shifted the emphasis to the political process including the role of the political party. They examined the effects of changes in party and convention rules and traced the connection between changes in the nominating process and the political process. Both have been participant-observers in the nominating process and thus were able to put forth the views of "physicians close to the patient in the bed."

1

It is no exaggeration to say that Herbert Alexander has devoted most of his professional life to the study of money and politics. The chairmen of the Miller Center commission on the nominating process had called on him both as a governor and expert witness whenever the issue of campaign financing was raised in their deliberations. Few can match the breadth of knowledge he has acquired as Director since 1958 of the Citizen's Research Foundation and Executive Director of the Presidents Committee on Campaign Costs in the early 1960s. His is the only presentation in the three volumes to throw the spotlight on money in the nominating process.

The issue of electoral reform vs. continuation of the present system in its broad outline remains unresolved. Richard M. Scammon stands in the front ranks of those who favor full play of the political process. Widely experienced in the workings of politics and co-author of fourteen volumes of *America Votes*, Scammon places confidence in the freedom of grassroots voters and political groups to pursue independent interests and make free choices. Sometimes as a lone voice, he speaks out against more ambitious constitutional and electoral reforms particularly those having to do with changing the time frame of primaries. He puts "brains and guts" ahead of all other qualifications for a presidential candidate.

The hallmark then of the present volume is its attempt to bring the discussion of the nominating process back to certain fundamental historical, constitutional, economic, and political issues. For the contributors, these issues persist and take priority over broad or narrow concepts of reform or the current controversies about the theory and practice of the nominating process.

'TIS DONE—BUT, 'TIS NEVER DONE

Alexander Heard

My appreciation for Kenneth Thompson's invitation to give a George Gund Lecture is three-fold. I am much aware of the diverse and important attention that the Miller Center has been directing to the American presidency and am complimented by the chance to take part in its deliberations. I am also grateful for the privilege of speaking in this unique and famous place, one of the notable creations of the genius of our third President. And also I think of my friend Burkett Miller of Chattanooga and Miami.

In performance of official duty I sought Burkett Miller's generosity for Vanderbilt. Alas, his feelings about this university ran deep. He reversed the tables and enlisted my help in working out conditions under which his money could go for the purposes he wished and also be acceptable to the university. At one point he said, doubtless exaggerating, "I'll give them the money for an institute under the conditions they propose only if you will leave Vanderbilt and become the director." I was sure he had not cleared that proposal with higher authority. I am not sure he thought there should be one.

Because of those long conversations many years ago I have felt special kinship to the White Burkett Miller Center and have presumed to claim (in my private thoughts) a tiny bit of credit for its successful establishment. I have also thought that my friends Edgar Shannon and Frank Hereford should have funneled at least a small agent's fee to Vanderbilt.

Old friends are here this afternoon, to some of whom I am much indebted, and I am grateful for your interest and for your courtesy in coming. The old friends will know what I want to be sure all friends here know. I am a resurrected political scientist who was out of play for some twenty years as chief officer of a university. Much to my surprise, I now find myself not retired to enjoy the rewards of a long and virtuous life, but back at the books.

The Alfred P. Sloan Foundation invited me in 1980 to take a long look at what it called the "United States presidential selection process" and to suggest how to improve it. I have been taking that long look as my main occupation since July 1, 1982. With Divine Grace, my colleagues and I will have produced a manuscript for a book by June 1985.

In 1981, I had a series of four dinner meetings from coast to coast, mostly with politicians and journalists to get appraisals of the ways we presently nominate and elect our Presidents. In the summer of 1982, colleagues and I held a week-long conference at Montauk Point, Long Island, with two dozen persons, mostly political scientists and historians, to get help in identifying issues and framing the topic. Last spring we commissioned two dozen papers on varied aspects of the subject, some very general and some very precise, a substantial number of which have now come in. We have other consultations planned. In all of this I am supported by two research associates, trained political scientists both, Kay Hancock and Scarlett Graham, and a research assistant, Tom Underwood, and an administrative assistant, Susan Gotwald. If anything comes of it all, they will be the reason.

This is a way of telling you that we are nearer the start than the end of our undertaking at Vanderbilt, or at least of my full participation in it. We have reached no irrevocable conclusions nor cosmic solutions and I have no slate of recommendations to propose this afternoon. I feel as Washington Irving did in his preface to a journal reporting *A Tour of the Prairies:* "It is a simple statement of facts, pretending to no high wrought effect." We here know that few statements of fact are, in fact, simple, but it will be clear that today we are not pretending to any high wrought effect.

That will not surprise the many people here who are far ahead of me in commanding this subject. I am much aware that some two hundred books have been published on one aspect or another of presidential selection during the past fifteen years and the cascade is not abating. I will report the state of our thinking and welcome your reactions and suggestions.

On July 9, 1788, Benjamin Rush of Pennsylvania wrote: "'Tis done. We have become a nation . . . . (A)mple restitution has at last been made to human nature by our new Constitution for all the injuries she has sustained in the old world from arbitrary government . . ."[1] In ten months enough states had ratified the Constitution for the new nation to begin the task of creating itself. Two centuries later we are still at it.

The avenues to the American presidency have been altered more than any other constitutionally prescribed aspect of our political system. Constitutional amendments have changed the fundamental procedures for choosing Presidents and vice presidents, including the guarantees of who may take part. Also radically modified have been extralegal, informal and private processes that are part of presidential selection. Taken altogether, changes affecting presidential selection have, in fact, been more frequent and more extensive than changes in any other major part of our governmental structure. And the national ferment illustrated by the Gund Lectures, and otherwise in the work of the Miller Center, promises that the current accelerated attention to change in presidential selection, and in the presidency itself, will persist on our national agenda.

Adoption of the Constitution by the states in 1787 and 1788 was no easy passage. Lord Bryce concluded ninety-five years ago that had the decision lain with the electorate in each state voting on the same day, instead of with conventions deliberating over an extended period, "the voice of the people would probably have pronounced against the Constitution."[2] That thought is sobering. In 1787, a small group of fifty-five tested, influential leaders worked by explicit policy in secret. Unobserved by others, they went boldly beyond their instructions to recommend revisions in the Articles of Confederation and created a new kind of Constitution for a new kind of nation, and then saw it approved.

Our nation's constitutional functioning two centuries later is increasingly strained by fundamental, elemental changes in the nation's life. Now, in contrast to 1787, our political values, popular expectations, and often legal stipulations require exposed deliberations and a consequent popular influence on constitutional adjustments.

The new Constitution proved remarkably adaptable to changing expectations and circumstances. Enduring values were articulated and protected, notably by the first ten amendments. But in a sensitive, central matter, the way the President would be chosen, one that the framers dealt with haltingly and by a special process for compromise, the Constitution has been mercifully both restrained and malleable. The changes in law and practice have extended across the whole life of the nation, which fact carries a special irony. Despite the disputatious deliberations that led to the way of choosing Presidents that was finally prescribed in the Constitution, Alexander Hamilton opened the sixty-eighth *Federalist* paper with his much noted observation that: "The mode of appointment of the Chief Magistrate of the United States is almost the only part of the system, of any consequence, which has escaped without severe censure, or which has received the slightest mark of approbation from its opponents."

Modifications since the eighteenth century in the way American Presidents are chosen have stemmed from many sources.

The potential for deadlock, or alternatively for manipulation, was considerable under a system in which each elector in the electoral college voted for two persons without specifying one for President and the other for vice president, as provided originally in Article II. The anomaly became evident early. A President's chief rival would become his vice president and hence his possible successor. As the linking of political interests developed into factions with a degree of continuity and cohesion, the arrangement was clearly unsatisfactory. The Twelfth Amendment to the Constitution, adopted in 1804, provided for the separate election of the President and vice president in the electoral college, thus making factional and later party slates possible, or inevitable.

It is emphasis misplaced, however, to stress—as sometimes is done—that only once since ratification of the Constitution has an amendment been adopted, referring to the Twelfth Amendment, that substantially altered the method of electing the President. The substance of presidential selection processes has been directly affected by nine amendments subsequent to the twelfth.

The Fourteenth Amendment invalidated the three-fifths compromise of Article I by apportioning United States representatives among the states on the basis of a population that included former slaves (but excluding, still, those untaxed Indians). That amendment therefore altered representation in the electoral college as well as providing, among many other fecund provisions, that no state should abridge the privileges or immunities of citizens of the United States, the pertinent intended ones here being black.

The Fifteenth Amendment bore directly on the electoral

process by declaring the right to vote shall not be denied on account of race, color, or previous enslavement.

Women's suffrage was guaranteed by the Nineteenth Amendment.

The Twentieth Amendment deals extensively with presidential succession under special circumstances. The Twenty-Second declares that no person may be elected President more than twice, or under a certain condition more than once. The Twenty-Third gave the District of Columbia the right to participate in presidential elections. The Twenty-Fourth said no person could be prevented from voting for President or vice president in any primary or other election for failure to pay a tax. The Twenty-Fifth Amendment treats extensively and importantly presidential disability and succession and the Twenty-Sixth protects persons who are eighteen years of age or older from being denied the right to vote because of age. These ten amendments—and constitutional interpretations by the courts—have altered in consequential ways our selection of Presidents.

Congressional enactments have also addressed presidential selection. Procedures for selection of a President by the House of Representatives were adopted in 1825. An important statute was adopted in 1887 as a belated aftermath of the Hayes-Tilden controversy of 1876. It regulated the counting of electoral votes in the Congress. Congress has also enacted three presidential succession laws—in 1792, 1886, and 1947.

The first, passed by the 2nd Congress on March 1, 1792, provided for succession (after the vice president) of the president pro tempore of the Senate, then of the speaker of the House; if those offices were vacant, states were to send electors to Washington to choose a new President. Moreover, if a presidential vacancy or disability occurred at a time when there was no vice president and when more than six months of the presidential term remained, the contingent successor would act as President only until a new President and vice president could be chosen in a special election conducted under the electoral college method used for regular elections. The maximum period of contingent successor could serve was 17 months.

Almost a century later, passage of the Presidential Succession Act of January 10, 1886, changed the line of succession to run from the vice president to the secretary of state, secretary of the treasury and so on through the Cabinet department heads, in the order in which their departments had been created. The 1886 law excluded the two congressional posts from the line of succession and "appeared to give Congress discretionary authority to decide whether to call a special presidential election, and, if so, when."[3]

That law stood until Congress enacted the third presidential succession law on July 18, 1947. It is still in force. It placed the speaker of the House and the president pro tempore of the Senate (reversing their order in the 1792 law) ahead of Cabinet officers in succession after the vice president. In this Act, Congress rejected the idea of a special election in the event of a double vacancy in the presidency and the vice presidency. For the first time, a contingent successor was directed to serve "until the expiration of the then current presidential term," and the speaker (or the president pro tempore) was required to resign both his legislative leadership post and his seat in the chamber as a condition of assuming the presidency.

State governmental regulation has significantly shaped presidential and vice presidential selection. So has action by the political parties at both state and national levels. Especially conspicuous has been the enactment of diverse state presidential primary laws, beginning in Florida in 1901. Their use has expanded, contracted, and expanded again in irregular patterns during the eight decades since. The composition and conduct of national nominating conventions and their decisiveness in choosing candidates have seen much change, too. And, of course, campaigning has altered with technology, especially with changes in transportation, communication, opinion polling, and the ability to manipulate data. Political technology radically affects costs. The price in constant dollars per voter long was generally stable, but has risen startlingly during the last two decades. Sources of money have altered with the new impacts of government on a society of growing interdependence increasingly subjected to public regulation. The ultimate significance of the dramatic innovation of federal campaign subsidies is uncertain. The undesirability of the several thousand newly developed political action committees, mostly active in congressional elections, however, seems certain.

These are far from all the modifications of law and practice that have been made affecting presidential selection processes since 1788. They are enough, however, to back the contention that the ways and context of presidential and vice presidential selection have evolved steadily, importantly, and with diversity throughout our history and continue to do so.

Many of these changes during the first two centuries of our government's life can be attributed directly to the flawed nature of the original plan. Those who under pressure of time wrote the procedures for electing the President that were embodied in the Constitution of 1787 thought segmentally. They framed provisions to keep the President and Congress independent of each other in certain ways. They sought to insulate the way of choosing the President from the threat of faction or manipulation. They devised a plan that struck an acceptable balance between the interests of the large and small states. And they conceived of a presidency filled by a wise leader possessed of lofty insight into the requirements of a nation that had certain, albeit limited, common interests. The prospect of George Washington as the first President, acknowledged or not, pervaded conceptions of the office. But the system established for choosing a President did not satisfy the needs of the system established for governing the country. It addressed only part of the equation. Consequently, the presidential selection system was modified early and has been adapted continuously to the evolving values, circumstances, and political expectations of the nation. Changes in the national environment of presidential selection have stimulated modifications well beyond those readily attributable to flaws in the original selection plan.

The impulse to continue in that reform tradition persists today. Expressions of dissatisfaction with the observable, external characteristics of the process are frequent and widespread. They focus on the declining rate of voting among Americans; on the growing length of presidential campaigns; on increasing campaign costs; on the apparent superficiality of television-centered electioneering; and on the lessened cohesion and fuctions of the political parties. Some lament, while others applaud, that presidential and vice presidential nominees are no longer named by deliberative, negotiating processes within the national conventions. And a few applaud, while most deplore, the increasingly personal political campaigns of candidates conducted independently of the political parties.

Michael Barone wrote in the *Washington Post* last February 27, "The Democratic candidates for president are starting—actually, they started some time ago—on the longest obstacle course in quest of the leadership of a nation since George IV waited 23 years for his father, King George III, to be declared mad .... Many of the things they have to do to win the

9

Democratic nomination will work against them in the general election. Many of the things they do in the campaign will work against them if they become president . . . ."

David Broder had written on June 5, 1980 in the *Washington Post*: "There is a sense that something has gone terribly wrong."

Underlying this kind of discontent with the process are deeper anxieties over the state of the nation's governance. The long-established two-party system decreasingly performs its traditional mediating functions. The proliferation of highly organized, well-financed special interest groups disrupts the representative functions of representative government. Government's ability to deal successfully with the nation's problems is not seen to be keeping pace with the mounting numbers and varieties of problems it is expected to address. Since 1932, the role of the national government has expanded qualitatively as well as quantitatively. It has undertaken new functions.

Presidents especially are weighted down by the new burdens. The presidency has become the converging point for those increased governmental responsibilities. It is also the place to which the public's dissatisfaction with their discharge is directed. Presidents, feeling unable to satisfy all the expectations centered on them, engage in what Sidney Blumenthal calls the "permanent campaign."[4] Presidents now routinely use the political consultant's tools, especially sophisticated polling. They take what they learn of the public's perceptions of them to shape carefully crafted television and radio presentations, to launch direct-mail efforts, and otherwise to seek mass support for themselves and their programs—not just for purposes of the next election, but as a method of governing.

When public support wanes, presidential effectiveness declines. We have one-term Presidents because it is authentically difficult for a President to satisfy the hopes of a sufficiently large number of voters to get reelected. Defeated Presidents leave office enjoying low public esteem. Presidents don't look like the giants our early political socialization led us to think they should.

We thus have twin discontents: with the process of presidential selection and with perceived shortcomings in governmental performance. We are easily tempted to seek improvements in the latter by changing the former. The cry is heard, "If only we had a process that gave us Presidents who are more knowledgeable, more experienced, more stable, politically better armed to

10

lead . . . ." As part of the syndrome, enhancing presidential effectiveness is seen as an avenue to increasing general success in governing. It clearly is not enough, however, in the struggle toward that goal, to ask only how our methods of producing Presidents can be improved. More is required than "getting better Presidents," however defined. And it may even be that the presidential selection process cannot be engineered to produce reliably whatever we might agree "better Presidents" to be.

Yet, effectiveness in government is a requisite for citizens of a democratic republic. Hamilton wrote in the seventieth *Federalist* paper that "a government ill executed, whatever it may be in theory, must be, in practice, a bad government." While we expect effectiveness, it is the essence of constitutional democracy to limit the means available to government for achieving effectiveness. In the twilight years of the eighteenth century, the framers believed it possible to have effective government that would concurrently preserve our liberty and maintain republican bearings. These aspirations could be conceptualized as antagonistic to each other. They could be accommodated successfully in a system of government only if appropriate institutional arrangements could be devised.

The basic skeletal structure of the institutions they settled upon for combining these unfriendly objectives remains essentially as it was. Probably we should not be surprised that the effectiveness of government in mastering the problems it has taken unto itself over the subsequent two centuries is more and more criticized in many quarters of American society. Have the problems with which American constitutional institutions must deal so changed that the basic institutional design initiated in the Constitution is no longer able to accommodate both effectiveness and liberty, and the changing notions of what each of those concepts embraces? Is it possible that while the basic institutional profile has remained intact, subtle, cumulative changes occurring within the basic structure have diminished the capacity of the system to perform effectively? Is it possible for any set of institutions, however arrayed, to continue to combine liberty and effectiveness in our increasingly interdependent yet, ironically, increasingly fragmented world?

On the front of the current issue of *The Center Magazine* appears a quotation from the interpreter of the American frontier, Frederick Jackson Turner. Turner said: "Other nations have been rich and prosperous and powerful. But the United

States has believed that it had an original contribution to make to the history of society by the production of a self-determining, self-restrained, intelligent democracy."

In the forbidding context of the late twentieth century, however, the challenge to achieve both effectiveness and liberty looms ominously. Yet the problem is as old as constitutional government. Frederick Watkins, in a 1940 essay called "The Problem of Constitutional Dictatorship,"[5] posed the dilemma in its sharpest terms. He placed it in the context of crisis—a clear and present danger to a society's survival.

Crisis has historically been the exceptional condition for the United States. We have survived those we have known, retaining or regaining our liberties and moving ahead. Even in today's dangerous world, a sense of crisis is not constant. If it were, liberal society would likely perish. As Watkins argues, "where the conditions of survival are persistently severe, absolutism generally tends to become the normal form of government."[6] The government of permanent crisis depicted by George Orwell in *1984* provides a graphic literary illustration of Watkin's analytic point. The challenges posed to free society by crisis are instructive in thinking about more commonplace tensions between liberty and effectiveness in government. Watkins writes:

> Legal restraints are bound at some time or other to stand in the way of effective political action. Other things being equal, it is clear, therefore, that absolutism will always tend to be more efficient than constitutional government.[7]

But he then quickly goes on to caution that "of all political fallacies none is more deceptive . . . than the . . . tendency to confuse absolutism with omnipotence . . . ."[8] All the same, Watkins acknowledges that effectiveness and liberty cannot always be joined to good result, the most apparent case being in time of crisis.

> When a man is trying to save himself from falling off a stepladder, he is not likely to give much thought to the dangers of over-exertion. When a social group is faced with an immediate threat to its existence it also cannot afford to calculate in terms of a very distant future . . . . There is no point in worrying about the future unless you are sure that you have a future to worry about.[9]

Fortunately, the United States still has a future to worry about and a plausible chance to sustain a political system that combines basic liberty with adequate governmental effectiveness. But this need not always be so.

We cannot wisely ignore perceptions that government is ineffective in dealing with large problems of our time, whatever the source of those perceptions. Political change can often be more easily accomplished in a crisis, but political change is needed in quieter times to avoid crisis.

How can the United States improve the effectiveness of its political system while retaining and enhancing its democratic values, its liberty? The question has been continuously with us in its modern form for half a century. It is being raised currently with new overtones of urgency and by disparate voices. Many of these voices speak of their hope for help through changing how we bring the nation's chief executive to office. Doing that forces the issues in presidential selection beyond the process itself.

Much said and written assumes that proper modifications in the way we choose Presidents can help repair deficiencies in presidential leadership. But we would not necessarily get adequate presidencies by choosing better Presidents. Presidents discharge their duties and pursue our dreams through a system of government and politics. The institutions of government and circumstances of politics as well as the means of presidential selection determine the effectiveness of Presidents. We cannot assume that by periodic adaptation in the selection process we can sustain the democratic values we cherish, ignoring the governing system whose principal leader it chooses and whose policies it affects.

To give perspective to those of us who have committed ourselves to the importance of presidential selection, and therefore to the importance of the presidency, I quote from Don K. Price's new book, *America's Unwritten Constitution—Science, Religion, and Political Responsibility*. It is one of a series of works sponsored by the Miller Center. Professor Price writes:

Through its committees, Congress had long since taken over a major part of the control of administration: its legislation determined the missions of executive departments and the pattern of organization and personnel systems, its appropriations systems controlled the details of expenditure, and its agent, the General Accounting Office, settled the accounts.

On the other hand, such administrative authority as the President had (or now has) is the result of action taken by the Congress to delegate to him, especially through its enactment of the civil service system, the budget system, and other procedures for planning and management. If the President has control over administrative matters it is not the result of the written Constitution but of delegation from Congress, either by enacting explicit statutes or by refraining from interference . . . . (E)ven if such delegation is granted by explicit statutory enactment, it may be withdrawn by informal political pressure . . . .[10]

It is the glory of the American Constitution that it has preserved and extended fundamental liberties that it sought in 1787 to guarantee. The magnitude of the transformation in our national life that would come with the two centuries following 1787 could not have been envisioned, yet the Constitution has proved to be hallowed with remarkable realism and to be capable of amendment with remarkable success. So far it has embodied a magic mixture of flexibility and constancy that has kept it viable.

The constitutional arrangements that evolved after 1787 did not prevent the Civil War three-quarters of a century later. Possibly no constitutional system could have assured a peaceful solution to the problems of slavery and their related economic and political issues. That is a reminder that nations have lives far deeper than their political structures and procedures and than their constitutions, written or unwritten. The resort to arms in 1861 demonstrated that the capacity of the constitutional system to force, or accommodate, social reform was limited. We do not now face the kind of divisive issue that brought violence then. But that experience is instructive. It demonstrated that evolving values deeply held and a radically altered social context could impose strains on the then existing American constitutional arrangement beyond its capacity to cope.

We have no way of calibrating finely the ability of the U.S. political system to accommodate stress. We do not know with certainty the limits to its capacity to make procedural, structural, philosophical adjustments to new burdens while sustaining old values. We do know, however, three things.

14

First, our democracy will not survive through an automatic process of adaptation. The hard work of creative intelligence diligently applied is needed in the twentieth century as it was in the eighteenth.

Changes in a political system, large and small, flow from competitive pressures. The incentives of some influential participants are always narrowly self-serving. Others will be moved by more general and less parochial incentives, by a concern for a large welfare over a longer run. Self-interest is always present, but the capacity for insight and the impulses of statesmanship are latent in many, perhaps most people. They can enlarge an outlook, letting it identify personal with national purposes. Watkins states the case pointedly:

> Nothing is more intensely human than a desire to have a cake and eat it too. In some cases where the connection between having and eating is fairly indirect, the demand can even be made to sound quite plausible and humane. ... Even though immediate concerns may tend to carry unusual weight, the fact remains that most individuals have a very real interest in the welfare of the larger community in which they live. In many cases it will be found to have a stronger emotional appeal than the particular interests with which it comes in conflict. Under these circumstances all that is needed to achieve unified national action is to make the issue between having and eating wholly clear and definite. This is one of the major tasks of contemporary statesmanship.[11]

We ought not rely passively on existing constitutional practices for future success. Nor should we depend solely on incentives for personal political advantage to spur adequate adaptations to our radically altered governing requirements. A larger vision of the American destiny is needed to animate what is to be done.

Second, we face a new order of challenge to American processes of self-government. The challenge is not provoked by a single intractable danger that must be addressed successfully or the nation will perish. It derives not from even so potent a new thing as nuclear weaponry, or so potent an old thing as the impact of technological innovation of the job market. Nor is the new order of challenge the consequence of a sudden, apocalyptic recognition by many of a life-threatening condition previously recognized by a few—like depletion of the underground water supplies on which our industries, our agriculture, and we ourselves are dependent.

We are confronted by a complex of interrelated phenomena that sum up to a gestalt, and it is that gestalt that is the new national condition. It is new in the multiplicity and interconnectedness of its origins, in its defiant complexity, and in its potential for worldwide societal disruption.

We have been moving toward this intensity of interdependence for at least four decades—or, more realistically, since the fifteenth century, or more realistically still, since the Garden of Eden.

It means that the presidency, and selection for it, has a new order of relationship to what happens outside the sphere of present U.S. politics and public policy, a new order of relationship to what happens far beyond American control among other peoples, in other nations, in other parts of the world.

Third, the critical question then becomes, put too narrowly, whether our evolving way of choosing Presidents can produce Presidents with attributes adequate to the evolving context of the office. The basic question is whether the process can produce *presidencies* adequate to our nation's needs.

The issue is fundamental. The overarching concern of the Constitutional Convention was the totality of the national government it would create. The failure of the founding fathers to devise a presidential selection system fully compatible with the structure and values of the new democracy led not to crisis or disaster but to early change. Americans need now to assess their presidential selection process in the perspective of the American constitutional system as a whole and that system's capability.

James L. Sundquist in 1980 described our condition compactly. He wrote:

> For in the last decade or two, the political scene has changed profoundly, and the changes all militate against governmental effectiveness.
>
> Four of the trends, all interrelated, affect the government's ability to formulate policy: the disintegration of political parties, the popularization of presidential nominations, the rejection by Congress of presidential leadership, and fragmentation of authority in Congress that

prevents its development as an alternative source of policy integration and leadership. A fifth trend is the graduate deterioration of administrative capability.[12]

Although how we nominate and elect presidents surely cannot be expected to carry the full burden of our federal life, much can be asked of it.

But it is essential to remember that services to be rendered or functions to be performed by a system for choosing Presidents do not match neatly features of structure or process so that by altering the latter, one can in predictable ways modify the former. Institutional changes have cross-cutting effects and processes and functions have multiple origins. That is one reason for the unintended consequences often precipitated by procedural and other formal changes in nomination and election procedures.

The ideal mode of institutional development is to define the values desired, hypothesize means to achieve them, adopt those means as policy, administer them as intended, and modify them in light of experience. But experience has taught that the process is more tangled than that. From the original provisions in Article II for choosing the Chief Magistrate through changes in party rules and statutes of the past decade, including the Federal Election Campaign Act Amendments of 1974 as interpreted, the difficulty of regulating electoral processes to achieve specified goals has proved mammoth.

It is not hard to articulate ambitions for our political system. We want effectiveness in coping with the problems thrown up by the changing conditions of the nation's life. We want to preserve democratic-republican values of participation in the political system as ends in themselves—but also, we insist, as instrumental in gaining greater governmental effectiveness over a longer run. We envision a presidency that is one part of a Madisonian web of government functioning not in opposition to, but in concert with, other political institutions, especially the Congress.

Our polity does not function, however, in generalities. Written constitutional provisions, congressional enactments, state statutes, and party rules, are shaped and twisted by judicial interpretation and administrative application. Competitive urges and ingenious initiatives both within the law and rules and in unregulated spheres contribute to unpredicted results. Powerful subliminal forces have shaped presidential selection from the very beginning, progressively converting it into an operation radically contrary to the founders' concepts. While the processes of exploitation and adaptation proceed as they always have, anxiety mounts as the danger and difficulty of the country's conditions increase. Can we still govern ourselves?

We are concerned to select the wisest, ablest leaders from those who present themselves for office. But we hold that all the individuals elected to office, plus all they call to help them, will not have the wisdom and information possessed by a whole society of individuals. That society turns to government for decisions, but it can provide information, intelligence, and creativity that may at times complicate decisionmaking but will in the end enhance the quality of the decisions. We hold that concept to be true. That fact itself helps to make it true.

A presidential selection process that encourages robust participation in politics, that facilitates exchange of information and opinion among the governed and their governors, that educates the electorate to the nature and possibilities of government, that contributes to national unity in the presence of diversity, that strengthens commitment to our democratic political life, can increase the likelihood that we will enjoy a government of both liberty and power.

It cannot guarantee effective governance. It cannot shield the United States from a world of threat and hazard. It cannot by itself settle the intractable substantive problems that beset us. It cannot guarantee prosperity or safety in an interdependent world of independent actors. But the process can contribute to our most important collective responsibility—governing ourselves well.

Good governments, self-governments, are never established once and for all time. In the sweep of human experiences they are creations. Their self-governing mechanisms often function differently than intended. That is a durable, vexing characteristic of democratic government. The Miller Center, and others in the ranks, must, nonetheless, hold steady in the effort to understand and improve. If good governments are to endure, their creation must be seen as done, but yet never fully done.

Footnotes

1. L.H. Butterfield, ed., *Letters of Benjamin Rush,* Volume I: 1771-1797: Princeton, Princeton University Press, 1951, p. 475.

2. *The American Commonwealth*: London, MacMillan and Co., 1888, pp. 31-34.

3. Allan Sindler, "Presidential Succession and the Vice Presidency," an analytic study commissioned for use in the study of the presidential selection process at Vanderbilt University, August 30, 1983, typescript, pp. 24, 30.

4. *The Permanent Campaign* (New York: Simon and Schuster, 1982; rev. ed.), p. 336.

5. In C.J. Friedrich and Edward S. Mason, *Public Policy— A Yearbook of the Graduate School of Public Administration, Harvard College* (Cambridge: Harvard University Press, 1940), pp. 324-79.

6. Ibid., p. 326.

7. Ibid., p. 325.

8. Ibid.

9. Ibid., p. 326.

10. (Baton Rouge and London: Louisiana State University Press), pp. 125-26.

11. *Public Policy,* pp. 373-374.

12. "The Crisis of Competence in Government," in Joseph A. Pechman, ed., *Setting National Priorities: Agenda for the 1980s* (Washington: The Brookings Institution, 1980), pp. 539-40.

THE POLITICAL AND NOMINATING PROCESS:

David Price
Albert Beveridge, III

MR. THOMPSON: We are very pleased that Mr. Beveridge and Professor Price could be with us. This is a continuation of the activity of the Miller Center in the area of presidential nominating politics. We began in the reverse order in a sense and we've tried to correct that with a forthcoming commission we have on presidential transitions and their impact on foreign policies. Fritz Mosher and David Clinton are writing a one-hundred page monograph with basic information about transitions and we have had some lectures and discussions here because the thought was that, if it were to have any impact at all, the commission report ought to get out quickly.

In the past we simply let the commissions take over and they held hearings with a large number of people but there was a minimum amount of discussion by academics and authoritative students of the problem. We were fortunate enough, though, in the nominating process report to have the ideal draftsman. Jim Ceaser drafted the report in record-breaking time, making use of the views of the commission, and in that respect I don't think we could possibly have come out any better than we did.

But we followed up as we did with the Press Conference Commission Report. You remember President Reagan's first press conference when James Brady appeared and held up the commission report of the Miller Center and said that the Reagan administration was going to follow the recommendations of that commission. To some extent they did especially as far as decorum and order is concerned. As for the recommendation of the second part of the report—regularity—there are different interpretations as to whether the commission report was followed. But in that case, as well as with the nominating process, we have held a series of roundtables and discussions

21

and had lectures and papers following the commission report. For instance, last week George Reedy, Jody Powell, and Jerry terHorst were here talking about the press secretary's view. A few weeks before that Frank Cormier, Helen Thomas, and Jim Deakin were here talking about senior White House press attitudes toward the presidency and the press.

In the same way we thought it would be important, and have tried to pursue this line, to have serious discussions on the nominating process. Volume I contained the discussions that went on last year, Volume II in 1983. We hope that our discussions this morning can be taped. We hope that your presentations can be incorporated in the third volume on the nominating process.

It is in that context that we brought a little group together to talk with the two of you who know a great deal about the subject. David Clinton, who is the Director of Special Projects at the Miller Center, will chair the meeting and introduce you and the subject.

MR. CLINTON: Thank you. I don't want to spend too much time on an introduction, just to repeat that we are delighted to have both of you here and to say that we are fortunate to have your views on this subject to add to some of the others that we have had up to now. Both of our speakers today did have service in connection with that other commission, the Hunt Commission, and if you want to speak on your experiences in that along with your prepared substantive remarks we would be delighted to hear that as well.

We will begin with Professor Price.

PROFESSOR PRICE: To begin our discussion, I will outline some of the ways the nominating system bears on party strength. It has often been claimed that changes in the presidential nominating system have, in various ways, sapped party strength, and that high on the agenda of commissions that are writing and re-writing the rules should be some attention to the strength of the party, the party as an institution. I agree with that. I think, however, that the linkages are not as clear as they are sometimes assumed to be. So it struck me that one of the ways to lay the framework for discussion would be to talk about the current state of the parties and how the nomination system affects that strength.

There is a huge literature now on the disintegration of the parties, the decline of the parties and the weakening of their hold. I don't really dispute the main drift of that literature, but in examining the question of party decline I think we do see some variations in different realms of party life. We might distinguish different aspects of the party and ask what some of the indicators of decline are in each, trying to become a little more precise in our diagnosis.

V.O. Key's traditional distinction is as good as any: party in the electorate, party as an organization, and party in government. Our estimate of party strength and of the state of the parties will differ according to which aspect of party life we're looking at.

The evidence is most clear when you look at the party in the electorate. There are several indicators that are commonly assumed, and I think rightly so, to show a loosening hold of party on its mass base, a decline in psychological attachments to the party and in the use of party as a cue in voting. Many studies show an increase in "independent" identification, more split-ticket voting, and other indications of the decline of the party's role in shaping and structuring electoral choice.

When you look at parties as organizations the evidence is somewhat more mixed. We typically look at the functions the parties fill, the kind of resources they command. On those kinds of measures there are clearly declines at virtually every level of party life: the decline of patronage at every level, the decline of the party's role in staffing the government, the decline of the incentives it has to offer its own workers and its own members, and a decline in the party's campaign management role—management as opposed to campaign services. Almost nowhere now do the parties actually come in and run the campaign. They are at best a kind of adjunct operation. There is a decline, of course, in party control of nominations at all levels, stemming most decisively from the advent of the direct primary, now fueled by all sorts of other developments.

There is some resurgence, as John Bibby's research team at Wisconsin has pointed out, in the institutionalization of the parties at certain levels.[1] In state after state, and certainly at the national level, parties are raising more money, have more staff, and are performing a wider range of services. The cold campaign management function may be in decline, but campaign services are on the rise. The kind of thing we've been able to do in North Carolina is not atypical. We now have a state Democratic party operation that has a half-million dollar budget even in an off year, has extensive computerized operations for targeting and voter registration and backup services for get-out-the-vote, polling and other kinds of campaign services. That's not atypical. There is an organizational comeback underway at the state level that complicates the picture of party decline. At the national level, of course, such organizational development has been most conspicuous in the Republican party.

When you turn to party-in-government I think the evidence is also mixed, although probably more on the negative side. There is some resurgence in party voting in Congress; it's hard to know exactly what explains that. I think it is something more than just a temporary phenomenon of the first Reagan year. Actually since the mid-seventies there has been a rather steady upward climb in levels of party cohesion, in party polarization in Congress. There has been a strengthening of leadership functions; the whip system is now more developed than it has ever been and from all accounts this is having some effect. Certainly the people working there think that it does. There is a policy role that Gillis Long and the Democratic caucus have carved out for themselves which I think is a very interesting experiment, something we've not seen on the Democratic side for a long time. Chuck Jones, of course, has written about a similar effort on the Republican side twenty years ago.[2] There is some stirring of the parties in Congress, but these attempts to bring the parties back are starting from a very low base-point. There is a basic situation of fragmentation and of individual electoral entrepreneurship in the Congress that basically is not amenable to strong party leadership. Party leadership in Congress is operating in a fundamentally hostile environment.

In state legislatures you find wide variations, but the general trend is toward loosened party control. And as you look at executives, both national and state, you see what Joe Califano has termed an increasingly "apartisan" executive. Califano's chapter by that title[3] is based mainly on the Johnson administration, and Nelson Polsby has shown the declining regard for party in presidential cabinet and other top-level appointments more recently.[4] The President has developed his own machinery for legislative liaison and now for liaison with interest groups, in many ways displacing past party functions. Similar trends are evident at the state level. That literature is very spotty, but various recent studies of the governorship show that, except in their legislative operations, governors are more and more inclined to detach themselves from the party, both in campaigning and governing.

24

So, when you look at the party in its various aspects it is not a simple thing to analyze. There is not any glib generalization one can make. The parties are in a state of flux, their traditional roles are in decline, and the emergence of new roles and new resources is still uncertain. It is a mixed picture, and only in some respects a promising one. I'm obviously operating from the premise that we have something important to lose if the kind of cohesion and accountability that parties have brought to government decline further.

What about the impact of the nomination system? From McGovern-Fraser forward, can we generalize about the impact of that line of reform on the parties? I think in general we can, although some of those linkages are not as clear to me as they seem to be to others. When you look at the party in the electorate, it is very hard to say anything very definitive about the impact of reform. What critics of the McGovern-Fraser and successive commissions often overlook is the real crisis of legitimacy that the system faced, at least on the Democratic side, in the late sixties. Something had to change. Had those changes not occurred, there would have been an increasing likelihood that the McGovern candidacy or something like it would have taken place outside of party channels. One can argue that there were positive effects of reform from the standpoint of the party's legitimacy, from the standpoint of its hold on certain constituencies within the party. On the other hand, one would be very hard pressed to argue that reform has notably increased the party's legitimacy across the board, or psychological attachment to the parties. Most such indicators in fact suggest that party "decline" has continued unabated. So it is hard to argue that party reform has really strengthened the party-in-the-electorate, although it is not as easy as it is sometimes assumed, I think, to make the opposite case.

The case is clearer for the party in its more institutionalized forms. There are three primary areas in which one can identify a generally negative impact. The first is very familiar—the proliferation of primaries. A lot of ink has been spilled debating to what extent the reforms actually bear responsibility for that development. Up to a certain level primaries can be useful, for testing the waters and so forth, but when we get to the point where three quarters of our national delegates are allocated through the primaries we have a system where major functions have been taken away from party organizations, and where the party has lost a major element of control.

25

Secondly, the removal of elected officials from the nomination process. I don't think anyone disputes that that has taken place, or that the Democratic rules established by the McGovern-Fraser and Mikulski commissions contributed to the decline of convention participation by public officials. Republican elected-official participation has remained steady over the entire period, while Democratic figures have fallen off drastically. There are two major reasons for that: these people have to run against their own constituents for delegate positions, and they have to declare their presidential preference months in advance. Both of these conditions represent very strong disincentives. To try to become a delegate under those circumstances obviously is going to appear politically damaging.

The absence of these officials hurts the party. They feel less involved in and responsible for the platform the convention adopts and the nominee it chooses. The presidential candidates have less reason to seek out alliances with the party's leaders and officeholders. Both the party in government and the party as an organization are weakened as a result.

Thirdly, there has been a reduction in the authority of party conventions and caucuses and the role of party organizations all up and down the line. Most obviously, there has been a reduction in the discretion and the power of the national convention. The Democratic Convention in 1980 was a "bound" convention. The Hunt Commission modified the binding rule, but didn't really change the situation fundamentally. The convention is basically locked in by the primary system and by the system of candidate approval of those who wish to run for delegate. The convention has very little flexibility. That, I think, is a net loss for the party in terms of its authority and the quality of the decisions it is able to make.

There has been a similar loss of authority and loss of resources by party bodies down the line. State conventions, district conventions increasingly simply ratify primary outcomes. They are often dominated, or even replaced, by candidate caucuses. Even such things as who gets to go to the national convention are now largely under the control of the candidate organizations and constituency groups within the party.

In these three respects, if not others, one can argue that the reform regime has weakened the party, certainly the party in government and the party as an organization. Functions have been displaced and resources have been depleted. That points, I think, to a "decline," and one that will not easily be reversed. It seems to me that party rules-writing bodies ought to pay more attention to the overall state of the party and ought to become more self-conscious about attempting to apply correctives.

Finally, let me close by reflecting on the extent to which the Hunt Commission was able to apply such correctives. I'm not suggesting that everybody or even most people on the Hunt Commission were making their decisions with this kind of party-strengthening framework in mind. There were many, many agendas around that table, and the fact that we were able to do some things that moved in the desired directions did not owe as much to conscious thinking about these problems as to a fortunate convergence of interests. We can discuss the politics of the commission later if you want.

But whatever the motivations, whatever the reasons, I do think that some of the things the Hunt Commission did are promising. To take those three areas of difficulty that I lined out: I think in one of them we had a major impact, in one we had a marginal impact, and in one we had almost no impact. Let's start with the washout, the primary problem, a very difficult problem. We did almost nothing about that. There was some talk. For Donald Fraser and Douglas Fraser, this was number one on the agenda, Doug Fraser representing a major segment of the labor movement and Donald Fraser speaking for a certain kind of long-term reformer, although he's hard to pigeonhole, a very interesting man. Anyway, both of them came in saying primaries ought to be on top of the agenda and let's do whatever it takes to get the number of primaries down, or at least to reduce the number of delegates that are committed through primaries.

The scheme that both of them were toying with was putting a cap on the percentage of a state's delegates that could be committed through a primary process. A quick footnote on how that might work: You might say, for example, that no more than 75% of a state's base delegation (excluding the elected officials and other "add-ons") could be committed through primaries. This would be the simplest form for such a plan. For most states, the simplest way to implement it would be to say that the delegates you're selecting at the district level would be allocated according to the primary result. But for the at-large delegates you're picking at the state level, you're going to have to devise some other method of allocation, presumably some kind of caucus/convention selection culminating at the state convention.

The two Frasers thought that such a plan would, first of all, be so complicated and so difficult that a number of states might rethink the whole idea of a primary. And secondly, they thought it would contain the damage in the sense that, if a state wanted to have a primary, at least there would remain some important function for the organized party. The commission thought about these schemes and appointed a group of experts to look at them and ended up deciding that they were too complex and too coercive to adopt. I suppose I shared that judgment, although reluctantly. They really would complicate the process enormously, and would be greatly resented. It is just a very difficult problem. There has been some leveling off, however. I think three states now have canceled their primaries for 1984. The upward trend in the number of primaries may have stopped. Many of the remaining states have well-established caucus systems, and some of our rules have created marginal disincentives for certain kinds of primaries.

Still, the leveling off has taken place at a very high level. National rules can't really turn the trend around, although it would be nice if it could be done. It is not clear what kinds of devices are available to us.

Now the second area, where we effected marginal changes: the discretion and authority of party organizations and conventions. By including more elected and party officials, we've given the state parties more leverage in making up the state delegations, marginally increasing their resources and their discretion. And we've given the national convention slightly more flexibility by adding a group of unpledged delegates and removing that binding rule that provoked such a fight in 1980. But our efforts to loosen up the system further were unavailing. There were a number of people on the commission, mainly representing the state parties, who would have liked very much to begin to dismantle this apparatus whereby candidates can basically slate their delegates. It is a complex apparatus that virtually is foolproof for the candidates. In some three different ways they can guarantee that their people are slated and are elected as delegates. Their control over the process is virtually complete, except for this small group of unpledged delegates over which the state parties may have more control.

Attempts to loosen that up were unavailing. We ran up against the interests of the candidates, and the interests of organized labor, who would rather negotiate with the candidates than with the parties. The only thing we did was get rid of the binding rule which, as I say, is an improvement. It could be important in a critical situation, where there were major changes, major upheavals that made it imperative that delegates reconsider their commitments. But what we did does not really alter the convention's or the party's role.

On the third problem, the absence of the party establishment from the convention, we did make some important changes. They did not go as far as many of us, including Governor Hunt, would have preferred, but we did provide for a substantial block of uncommitted delegates, who can give the convention some flexibility and, more importantly, can participate in its deliberations and help unify the party for purposes of campaigning and governance. I don't want to oversell that. We tended to oversell it simply because we were trying to get it passed, and we were putting a strong face on our efforts. I've no illusions about what it will do. I don't expect party-voting rates in Congress to soar by virtue of these people having gone to the convention. However, I think it is a positive move and it's one that, combined with other things that are happening with the parties in Congress, may have some effect.

Now, there are a couple of other things we did. Let me refer to them in passing and close. It is hard to argue that they did much for party strength one way or the other. The first one is looking more and more dubious—that is, shortening the campaign season and reducing the disproportionate impact of Iowa and New Hampshire. I should say, actually, that the second objective, reducing the disproportionate impact of those small early states, really was higher on the agenda for most people than simply shortening the season per se. "Shortening the season" became a kind of euphemism for making the process more representative. No one wanted to seem to be berating New Hampshire and Iowa too much, so they spoke in more general terms.

I do think, as to reducing the isolated impact of those early contests, that there will be some slight change. They will be treated by candidates and by the media more in conjunction with other contests. I think we've seen that already. Still, there's no question everyone is going to New Hampshire and to Iowa. There is some value, I think, in those early contests, but their isolated impact will be marginally reduced.

As to the length of the season, obviously we haven't had much impact on that. It is hard to argue that there is a clear-cut party stake in that. In terms of the party-in-the-electorate, the party's mainstream appeal, there is a case to be made for reducing the impact of those early contests. And insofar as we've done that I guess we made a positive move but I wouldn't want to stake too much on it.

The second change was in the proportional representation structure. We can discuss that later if you want. A lot of people have argued that in getting away from strict proportional representation you strengthen the party, helping it coalesce around a mainstream candidate that is responsive to the large industrial states and to the party's core constituencies. Probably, that is true, but there again, I wouldn't want to stake a whole lot on that argument.

Then we left one major problem unresolved, and I think that one really does have implications for the party that we barely discussed. That is the problem of what has become known as "front-loading." I think that the problem of New Hampshire and Iowa pales in significance beside the problem of states moving to early dates within the three-month campaign period, known as the "window." There are two things that this does. One, it devalues the process in the later states, many of which are large industrial states that ought to be the pivotal states in the system. And it makes it much harder to retain caucus systems, because if primaries are being held in March and are locking in delegations, and the caucus system cannot *begin* until March and needs about a two-month time frame to complete itself, then retaining the caucus system becomes more difficult. Final convention decisions will not be made until after the delegations are locked in from most states. Front-loading thus creates problems in terms of the impact of a range of states, and it could also create a powerful additional incentive to move from caucus to primary. Party regulars tend to dismiss the problem and see it as something that can't be very well addressed. There are some people who think we should deal with it, but they tend to be rather lonely voices. It is a major unresolved problem which I think is going to come back to haunt us.

Well, that's a very sketchy treatment, but I hope it has laid out some of the questions that one might think about in trying to work through this rather complex set of rules, and in trying to be a little more specific than we ordinarily are about the implications they have for the strength of the party.

MR. BEVERIDGE: I will sort of take a different viewpoint. That's because frankly I have not been a student of parties and the whole delegate selection process. I've been much more of a worker in the vineyard. My present role is counsel to the CRC, which as I'm sure all of you know, is the group within the party which reviews state delegate selection plans to ensure that the rules are followed. I was counsel to the Hunt Commission but I cut my teeth, as it were, first in 1968 with Robert Kennedy and then in 1972 as associate counsel to the Credentials Committee. And just from a personal viewpoint we are a lot better off now than '72. I recall that in 1972 we had the magnificent rule that if someone could get 15% of the Credentials Committee go along with him, he could present a minority report and virtually everybody was saying, "Sure, I'll vote for your minority report if you vote for my minority report." As it turned out on Tuesday, I think, from 2 until about 10 or 11 at night, all over national television we were arguing gay rights, we were arguing about some tribal council, anything some idiot group could get 15% together on. I thought that at least Tuesday night, which was the platform night, was an absolute disaster. Many say that the image of the convention was reflected in the results in 1972 but certainly, personally I thought was a very discouraging event. And we are in, I think, much better shape now.

What I thought I might do is first describe where, from the point of view of the CRC, we are now in the implementation of rules and some things that seem to be becoming apparent and then suggest a few personal, very personal—how should I say?—discouragements I had with the system. The nicest thing about the Hunt Commission, as far as I'm concerned, was meeting David Price so if I seem to be a little negative about the whole process it is certainly not a reflection of our executive director nor of Governor Hunt who was a great leader.

The first point I think I can make is that the rules are holding very firm. I was a little surprised at the depth of feeling in the DNC in wanting to uphold the rules. At the last DNC meeting there were two challenges to the existing rules. As we all know, you can appeal to the DNC to change the rules. There were two appeals. One was perennial and it may become now quadrennial appeal of Wisconsin to allow an open primary. The Governor is very much behind the open primary. He claims that it would be an absolute disaster, and that Wisconsin would never vote Democratic again, if it doesn't hold an open primary. And, the state sought a change to allow Wisconsin to have an open primary. That was defeated by voice vote.

The other appeal was a move by Mr. Fink, who is the leader of the Lower House in New York, to put state legislative leaders in a preferred category in terms of consideration. He pointed out, not unreasonably, that in some states the Senate Majority Leader or Speaker of the House may be the top Democratic officials, at least at the state level, and yet they are not specifically mentioned anywhere in the rules. That appeal was also defeated, but to my mind, what discouraged me, was the acrimony surrounding that entire issue. But I think it is fair to say that there is overwhelming consensus to enforce the rules within DNC.

On one of the issues that has been touched on, the primary versus caucus, the latest count that I get from our executive director is compared to 1980, when you'll recall there were 31 primaries and 25 caucuses. Now, I think it can be definitely stated there will be 25 primaries and 31 caucuses. That's not an insignificant shift. And, there are several others that are very possibly going caucus and will leave the primary route. I don't think much of it has to do with the rules of the party or anything to do with political science or anybody else saying how bad primaries are. I think the main driving force is money. It is expensive to hold a primary and many states are finding that unless there is a quid pro quo, either substantial involvement of the candidates in the process or some opportunity to make a substantial national impact, it isn't worth holding a primary.

As I indicated, my first political experience was in 1968 when I was sent by Kennedy's committee to Oregon. I was told, and had no reason to doubt it, that every four years the primary in Oregon in those days was the third or fourth largest industry in that state. Lumber, obviously, and fishing were larger, but it was an extraordinary event and I'm sure all of you who follow politics know that the Oregon primary was a huge boon to that state's economy. Now, I believe many states are finding that it is not worth the cost of holding a primary election.

In regard to primaries versus caucuses the other thing that seems to be taking place is the jockeying of the candidates. Major states like Ohio with a candidate like Glenn would like to reward its favorite son early in the process, perhaps through the use of bonus delegates or some other method. But, the only practical way for it to do so is through a caucus system because the Republicans are not anxious to help Democrats in rewarding a Democratic candidate.

So I don't think that the rules have done so much to change the system, economics is probably the strongest force.

One issue that David touched on was timing, and there, the prospect is discouraging. The candidates clearly are off as early as ever. I don't think we've seen any slackening of the push to go early. There is a tremendous pressure for states to move early. I mentioned Ohio. California is uncertain—its plans change almost weekly—it is clear state leaders want to be earlier in the press. However they are faced with a real dilemma. First of all, the Republicans will not go along with an early primary. Secondly, it is estimated that to hold a primary in California costs $34 million or more. And that is a lot of money to add to the state's budget when you are running a deficit. So they talk about caucuses, but then they are caught in a dilemma because if the Democrats hold early caucuses and the traditional Calfornia primary takes place there will undoubtedly be some initiatives on the ballot. And if none were planned, you can be sure that the Republicans or those who are even more conservative, will see that there will be initiatives on it. The Democrats are quite correctly worried that if you don't tie initiatives to a Democratic election the Democratic vote will fall off and some initiatives will pass that otherwise would not. So they are caught in a sort of dilemma in California. But there is clear pressure to get in as early as possible and perhaps one of the most discouraging aspects is that elected officials, specifically the House and Senate caucuses, which are going to elect members of the House and Senate want to jump the gun. Their first proposal was, as I understand, that they be elected in November of 1983. Well that fortunately was taken care of by the Charter which prohibits it. The compromise seems to be that the election will be held in January of 1984 which certainly violates the spirit of the rules. I won't go into the technical arguments that can be made for or against but the caucuses certainly have an argument that such an election complies with the rules which, of course, push it before any primary. A favorite expression that floated around the Hunt Commission is called "The Law of Unintended Consequences." I think that is a euphemism frequently for sloppy thinking, and I am afraid that in this case we may not have tied down the rule specifically enough on this particular issue.

Let me turn now to the things that trouble me and that I worry about and I hope some of you will address and discuss. First of all, I want to make it clear I'm excluding the Republican party from these speculations. That's because I don't know that much about the Republican party. And what I do know, at least in terms of party strength, suggests it has done an outstanding job. The Bliss/Brock leadership has been what I hoped for the Democratic party at least in terms of techniques.

One thing that does trouble me is what I would call the suzerainty of the national Democratic party over the states. It's very clear now that the national Democratic party has absolute suzerainty, and that's been confirmed by the Supreme Court twice in the last decade. There may be a couple of little issues remaining but it's clear the national party is supreme. I don't know what this does to state parties but I will tell you, and this is my sense of history, how offended I was to have state House and Senate members to the convention chosen without the approval of their own states. That was one of the issues that emerged in the Hunt Commission. As a result we have for the first time a group of delegates which are selected totally apart from any state mechanism. I've always thought of a convention as a profoundly federalistic process which states assembled with their own individuality and their delegates the product of their own rules. But here we have an outside force— admittedly closely tied to the state—which can select delegates without the intervention of the state in any respect except for a little nod since the caucuses are supposed to write the state chairs and ask, "Who would you like to have selected?" It seems to me it is a fairly short step to accepting the selections of other interest groups for party reasons, whether it be a minority group or any other interest group. The argument hasn't been raised yet but the issue is there. I'm not saying it is necessarily bad, but it certainly troubles me and I'm not sure it is a good development for the party.

What also discourages me is the method chosen by a national party to exercise its authority—specifically to rely on rules. I question whether any organization which relies heavily on rules can remain a dynamic organization. These rules, you know, change every four years which is something one must wonder about. Why cannot the rules be phrased in more general terms so that they can stand the test of time for more than four years. They are also increasingly complex. I do not know what that complexity means in terms of participation for the electorate. Perhaps it means very little, but they seem to my mind unnecessarily complicated.

At the start of the Hunt Commission I had hoped there

could be some simplification in the rules but I am afraid the Democratic party is very much I think like the federal government. For example, if there is a perceived problem with the Internal Revenue Code, you don't simplify. As you all know you add complexity. Party rules seem to be following that particular trend.

We have tried, of course, to take some steps to make the process a little easier, for example, model plans which will be sent to the states. But the trend toward complexity appears inexorable. It troubles me. Naturally, complex rules mean some sort of bureaucracy. It is clear to me that the bureaucracy, although not very large, still conducts a bureaucratic operation. It is clear from discussions with those who participated in this process in 1980, that many were offended by the authority of the staff to interpret the rules—a typically bureaucratic function. I think it is the intent of the present leadership of the CRC to restrain its staff. But the staff on the CRC was perceived in the eyes of many state party officials, as having inordinant power and authority over the state's method of delegate selection.

Then, of course, the tension these rules can create within a state are extraordinary. I'm not sure this is true, but I was told that in one state as a result of equal division it is unlikely that the newly elected governor of that state, a Democrat of course, will be a delegate. In his stead will go a newly elected 26 year old female state legislator, and that is the product of equal division. One can't say that result will follow for sure but it is one of the problems the CRC staff is wrestling with. The governor, of course, can attend the convention in some capacity but certainly, he won't be in a role that was intended. And then of course you also have the tension of the states versus the DNC. Now let's go back again, to the governor of Wisconsin who having been defeated in the last DNC meeting has come up with a new proposal that the Democrats meet in caucus in March and vote to accept the results of the April open primary. He seems to believe that this suggestion somehow meets the rules, but I'm afraid it doesn't no matter how sophisticated an attorney or sophist you are. But, the issue is as a party what are we doing? Why are we still fighting with Wisconsin over an issue 12 years old. Obviously it is very strongly felt in Wisconsin. There is no doubt that the DNC has the votes to uphold the existing rule but it seems to me—if I can use the expression—counterproductive.

Aside from the tension that is created by the rules another

35

obvious problem is that we do not have any effective sanctions. There is only one sanction, actually two. First, you don't seat the delegation, and that is, I think, politically like dropping an atomic bomb for a small incursion onto your territory. Second, the DNC could go in as a suprastate body and actually conduct the caucus or primary. What the Democrats have done is not to offer any carrot to offset the stick. We have no real incentive—I wish we did—that we can offer states to follow rules.

Presently, the best incentive anybody can think of is the location of a state's hotel in relation to the convention center and a state's seating at the convention. Now those are pretty small incentives.

There are other troubling problems, but they are really outside the scope of this discussion. In terms of party the whole AFL/CIO endorsement presents a great problem for the party. There is nothing much we can do about it, but it is a major issue. In addition the rhetoric coming out of the Chicago mayorality race and the role of PAC's in the political process strike me as extraordinarily anti-party. But, what troubles me most are the rules, and their complexity. I recognize that it was necessary to restore a sense of legitimacy to the delegate selection process. I really wonder, however, if we haven't gone a bit too far.

QUESTION: Do you thing that the rule changes in terms ex-officio member are sufficient, just in terms of numbers, to bring about a deliberative character to the convention at all?

PROFESSOR PRICE: I have problems with the notion of a deliberative convention in the first place. I think those people who have advocated that kind of convention have romanticized the traditional convention. That is not to say, though, that there is not something very important at stake. There was a kind of political bargaining and coalition-building that went on that was very important—although it often did not fit the term "deliberation." I think the number we added could make a difference in a very close contest, but is really not likely fundamentally to change the character of the convention. In a closely divided situation it could restore a certain measure of importance to the convention; that would count as a net gain, I think. I know Jim Ceaser has expressed his misgivings as to whether the convention is any longer equipped to play that kind of decisionmaking role, whether the convention could bear the weight. I'd like to talk about that if we could, but my basic point is that what we have done is not really going to

36

change the convention's decision-making role very much.

I would see the more important impacts in the kind of involvement that our rule facilitates for party and elected officials, and also the kinds of incentives it creates for candidates to engage in alliance-building, particularly with members of Congress and state officials. Changing the character of the convention would be nice if it could occur, but what we've done will be more important in encouraging certain kinds of coalition-building. I suppose I'm not as concerned as Albert is about the Congressional caucus. It seems to me that the role that we've given the Democratic caucus of the House and Senate is a kind of transition measure, not one that will be in the rules from now on. I certainly started out feeling pretty negatively about it. I think a lot of people did. It became clear, though, over the course of our discussion that (Rep.) Gillis Long and the House Democratic caucus were quite serious about this. And organized labor, in particular, was intrigued with the idea. So it had a political viability that we didn't think it had at first. And as we began thinking about what it would take to get the Congress to the convention, what it would take to really turn this pattern of nonparticipation around, it seemed that a caucus role of this sort had a certain potential, particularly since Long and his people were pushing it so strongly.

Why they wanted it is an interesting question. I wasn't ever sure I was completely aware of that. In a sense, the congressional leadership is looking for a middle range of sanctions. They are looking for small things, small positive things that they have to offer, and this kind of convention role is perhaps one such thing. I think it adds to their arsenal in an interesting way. To the extent they feel that way about it and can use it as a way of solidifying their own role, I see what we did as basically acceptable. I don't think there is any likelihood that it will be replicated with respect to other party caucuses. The idea that you would turn over the selection of governors, for example, to a Democratic governors' caucus, or likewise for the mayors or whatever, I think that would not occur. It seems to me that the congressional caucuses are unique within the party.

MR. BEVERIDGE: I want to make it clear that the congressional caucuses *per se* don't disturb me. There was a real movement in the Hunt Commission to have the caucuses send their names back to the state for veto or some other kind of aped twenty years ago that a small caucus in Iowa would become the key player in the campaign and yet it is very good mechanism for television. I'm just wondering if television really has made the rules irrelevant and neither of you have made reference to that aspect of the campaign.

MR. BEVERIDGE: Well, I think that if you suggest that the media is much more important than the rules, I won't disagree at all. I'm not sure, however, that it has made them irrelevant. There was a strong feeling in 1976 that the rules were a substantial asset to the Carter candidacy. And I think there is still a feeling that the rules and when I say rules it includes many aspects like fund-raising, make it difficult for a Howard Baker to run, or for a legislative leader who is devoting a great deal of time to his legislative duties to run. And it can't all be the media because a senator can command immediate media attention. There are other factors than the rules, but they nevertheless do have some significant impact on the process. Furthermore, if a party were really willing to take very strong measures which I think would include, as David pointed out, front-loading and similar problems the rules could have even more impact.

PROFESSOR PRICE: I think the rules make a marginal impact, but that one often can identify the direction of their influence. I think the changes we made, the whole package of changes, do reduce the possibility of some unknown candidate coming out of nowhere, winning in New Hampshire and Iowa and sweeping through the system. It is a marginal impact—I would agree to that—but I do think it's worthwhile trying to identify it. Of course this kind of question is not mainly what we've been talking about. What I was concentrating on was the way these rules influence the resources and the roles of the organized *party*. It is a rather different question to what extent they influence the quality of the nomination choice. We've dealt with that only incidentally.

QUESTION: Insofar as you talk about strengthening the party, you wouldn't say that the rules have been the primary factor at work? For example, on the state level you talked about the interest of the parties, fund raising, and control of the various techniques of campaigns.

PROFESSOR PRICE: No, I think there has been a substantial impact, and I identified three areas where I thought the impact had been very direct. But I don't think the rules are an all-important determinant of party strength. I think, in fact,

proval. Unfortunately, that was defeated by voice vote as I recall. Having uncommitted congressional delegates was, I thought, a pretty good idea, but I also thought the states should have been involved more directly in the selection.

QUESTION: You say the rules change every four years. What do you think of the prospects of any further rules changes that would increase the bargaining or compromise nature of conventions?

MR. BEVERIDGE: First of all I do not think the rules are going to change between now and May 4. Secondly, if we have a Democratic President the chances are very strong that he—depending on who he is—will look over and see what rules he wants for 1988, and in that sense the rules will change. If we don't get a Democratic President, I think once again somebody will say, "Well, let's look at the possible reasons," and inevitably in the Democratic party, the rules will come up. So I would suspect that there will be another commission in 1985 or 1986. What do you think?

PROFESSOR PRICE: I'm not so sure. Maybe I'm kidding myself, but it seems to me that, given other things that are happening with the National Committee, there is the possibility that we will not appoint yet another full blown commission outside the DNC structure. I certainly hope we will not. I would hope we could keep this thing at a lower key next time. Of course, there will be changes, but I don't know that they will be as extensive, and I would hope that the National Committee could handle this next time around—as of course the Republicans, every time but one, have done. They had one Commission like ours; otherwise they handled it in the RNC. I think we're to the point where that is at least thinkable.

QUESTION: I'm a bit troubled frankly by the Democrats' fascination with the rules and I'm wondering to what extent these rules are really important at all. I understand they are probably important for representational concerns within the party but in terms of candidate selection I'm not sure how much difference it makes whether you hold caucuses or primaries and when you hold them. There seems to be a dynamic at work here that is largely beyond the control of parties, and I'm speaking with respect to the way the media treat the campaign process so that whatever window you have governing the primary process you have a campaign starting now and immense attention given to the formal meeting in California last month. I don't think anyone would have dream-

that a lot of the critics tend to overplay them. Other things are going on, and the rules are one factor among others. But their effect on party organizations and the way they function is very real.

Let me just say one thing, though, about the Republican party. We've had a lot of these inter-party discussions in recent years. You've had some here, and there was a conference up at the Kennedy School which came at a crucial time in our process.[5] At these inter-party discussions, the Republicans tend to get rather pious about the way they leave the states alone, about how they respect the autonomy and the diversity of their state organizations. I think Albert and I and a lot of Democrats share misgivings about the extent to which we intrude in state party affairs and the legalistic nature of our intervention. The Republicans largely avoid that. They have pretty much a laissez-faire system with respect to state party processes. Even the rather minimal Republican rules are often not enforced. The most notable case would be their requirement that first-stage meetings be open to all party members in a jurisdiction. The national rule is a little vague on that, but certainly one interpretation would be that allowing only precinct committee members to participate is a violation of the national rule. Yet a current RNC Report indicates that something like a dozen states, more or less, use that kind of system. So even the minimal rules they have they often don't enforce.

But they do exert control in other ways, so I think some of that piety is a little misplaced. There are important sanctions which the national Republican organization has with respect to the way local candidates and local organizations run their campaigns. If you don't use their consultants, if you don't use their techniques, you often don't get the cash. So I don't think there is any less centralization in the Republican party than in the Democratic. I think that by and large theirs is a more productive kind of centralization, one that is more conducive to party strength. But it can have a hardball aspect of which some of the state and local parties are resentful.

MR. BEVERIDGE: That is the carrot that I was referring to. I think one of the problems of the Democratic party, at least on a national level, is that campaign assistance has been neglected and certainly the financial aspects of the party have been neglected for several years. As you undoubtedly know the Democratic party has made some generous but financially disastrous decisions by taking over the McCarthy, Humphrey, and Kennedy campaign debts. We didn't have any money. It would have been one thing if you had a lot of money and you could afford the largesse. But, when you're broke and make that kind of commitment it can be disastrous. So there has been much less in terms of financial resources the party could offer.

PROFESSOR PRICE: I was the director of the North Carolina party in the 1980 campaign. From the standpoint of the state party, the national committee staff looks like a bunch of enforcement officers that you have to come to terms with. But they don't have much else to offer. We went through a rather demeaning process of trying to get a little voter registration and get-out-the-vote money channeled our way. Even that seemed to be a very bureaucratic, rule-bound sort of process. We had to establish that we needed the money, and how we would use it, and to answer a lot of questions. And in the end, we didn't get the money. We were ready to strangle the national operatives who didn't have much to offer but who were very officious in sheperding what few resources they did have. There is a great deal of resentment between the national and the state levels of the party which I think isn't productive and which is largely rooted in the kind of legalistic role the National Committee has craved out for itself.

QUESTION: I'm a little bit rusty and remote from the front lines now, but going down to the Virginia Capitol during the recent legislature and talking casually with some Democrats, I found that they were thinking about the favorite son device for coping with some of these new rules, and thinking that other states might do the same thing. I'm wondering is that considered a serious possibility, that we might have a whole bunch of favorite son delegations and so on and get tied up at the next convention. How would the rules cope with that?

PROFESSOR PRICE: Well, that is said from time to time. I can't help believing that's unrealistic. It seems to me the whole thrust, not only of the rules but also of the way presidential campaigns operate these days in terms of the media and of resources that the nationwide candidates have, make a reversion to that kind of pattern highly unlikely. There have been a few people who have attempted it in recent years. Apparently Cranston is relying in part on that kind of base of support. Every indication was that he barely managed, even in his home state convention, not to be embarrassed. The pull of national forces is so strong now that it is very hard for state leaders to control the situation.

MR. BEVERIDGE: I think that is the point. The way the rules are written it is very hard for a relatively small group to control that process. For a true favorite son candidacy to emerge, you really have to get most of your state behind you. It isn't just a couple of hundred legislators and county leaders and so forth and so on.

PROFESSOR PRICE: Even favorite sons sometimes face unruly state situations where they have to go into a primary, as opposed to simply working out things with the party leader. There is also the likelihood that the convention is not going to be a bargaining situation. The convention is likely to be locked up in one way or another, so you might be simply throwing your vote away as opposed to giving yourself bargaining leverage. For a state to decide that they are going to hold out for a favorite son is a pretty large gamble. It looks too much like dealing oneself out of the process, I think, for it to be very tempting for many states.

MR. BEVERIDGE: And let's look at some of the other things the party has done away with. We have proportional representation now. There is no unit rule or a number of other devices that were used before to give your favorite son a big bloc, or a really potentially powerful force. With proportional representation, for example, you've attenuated, I think, the strength of the favorite son candidacy.

QUESTION: I want to ask a couple of factual questions and then make one comment. I wonder if you could explain how the Congress is going to choose a congressional caucus, choose the delegates, the exact process that will take place?

MR. BEVERIDGE: The meetings are taking place next Monday or Tuesday, to map out the strategy. They haven't established it yet, and I think it is fair to say it will probably be another month until we will have a pretty good idea of how it is to be done.

QUESTION: Then, I had this comment in listening to the Hunt Commission and how this thing has evolved. If you look at it historically you have this situation in which the rules of the Democratic party over the last fifteen or twenty years developed first in a way that seemed to take power away from the party officials in ways that seemed to be more democratic. But by the time you reach let's say the late seventies or early eighties then you have a reaction, a partial reaction within the party, or parts of the party, and then an effort to try and reintegrate the party leaders in, and try and give the party organization a little bit more power than it had under previous rules. The irony of the whole process viewed from the outside is that you use the same mechanism to try and strengthen the party, namely national rule-making authority, that was originally used to weaken the party. So, the process of trying to strengthen it doubles the intrusion of the national party into the entire process. It is almost regretable, it seems, that, looking at the matter historically, you have to use a means which is so at odds with the final end. Because I suppose the strength of the American parties has something to do with building the thing up from the state and local levels where people can feel some participatory bond.

I just wonder if anyone came up with the radical idea in this Commission that maybe the best way to strengthen the role of party leaders given that was one objective in the early eighties, was simply to do away with the entire national rule-making process from start to finish, simply wipe out the whole set of rules, with perhaps the sole exception that there would be no racial discrimination. There probably had been so many vested interests which had built up that such a change would have been impossible, but I was just wondering, in hearing your presentation, whether that might have been a wiser course to follow?

PROFESSOR PRICE: Well, it's even worse than you say because not only do we, in attempting to correct the problems, use national rule-making authority, which is maybe part of the problem, but it goes further than that. We use a quota, which is even more a part of the problem. There was a very amusing column which Mark Shields wrote right in the middle of all this. "A Kiwi For Your Quota" I think is what he called it.[6] He talks about how no one uses the word quota anymore. No one admits that we have quotas, so let's just call them Kiwis, which is some kind of extinct species or something, and go on from there. The point of the article was that much of this apparatus, once in place, has proved very resistant to change. And now, on top of it all, we come in and have yet another "disadvantaged" group, the public officials, who themselves need a "kiwi" and so we impose yet another restraint, add another percentage requirement.

I appreciate the force of your criticism. As you intimate, basically the structure is in place and there are a lot of vested interests in it. The Democratic party has gone very far down this path of writing comprehensive national rules. Someone who wants to correct some of the problems these rules have spawned has very little choice other than to simply rewrite the rules, as opposed to starting from scratch.

I do think there are some constructive things that could be done further to dismantle certain aspects of the process without the kind of radical surgery you suggest. I think there are ways in which the elected official participation could be loosened up further, made easier. There are ways in which the whole candidate approval apparatus could be loosened and partially dismantled. One thinks in such an incremental fashion out of necessity. The rules are simply not going to be dismantled; the question is how to revise them in such a way as to minimize the negative impacts.

MR. BEVERIDGE: I think that's true. If you want to dismantle rules you really don't appoint a commission with lots of people who are interested in those rules. Because some of the people who participate in such a commission make their livelihood from interpreting and advising people on these rules. So it certainly won't be a Hunt Commission which will tear the structure down. I think the only way it is going to happen is for state leaders say, "You, DNC, aren't giving us any quid pro quo; we get nothing from you except a lot of officious bureaucrats who tell us how to run our affairs, and we're going to defy you." That is why I pointed to Maine. It would be interesting if that state really sticks it to the party, since aside from running the election for the state party or rejecting the delegation, the Democratic party has almost no sanctions.

PROFESSOR PRICE: I do think there is an assumption which runs through a lot of these discussions which needs to be questioned—an assumption that state autonomy will invariably serve party strength. I think it is entirely possible that the cumulative effect of state practices will have a party-weakening effect. In other words, I don't really accept the notion that the only problem we're dealing with here is one of national rules and national imposition. There may very well be a kind of collective-good problem within the party in terms of the cumulative effects of state practices. So it is not evident to me that there is no positive role for the national party in addressing some of those problems. I think timing is one such problem. I'm concerned that we're heading down the road toward a national primary, and the most important single trend in that direction is the front-loading trend. The national rules have something to do with that, but states' calculations of their own interests also have a lot to do with it. I'm at a loss as to what to do to arrest that trend. But I don't rule out entirely some kind of policy role for the national rules—freezing certain portions of the calendar, etc. In other words, I don't think national rule making is inevitably a sign or a cause of party decline. You have to consider the possibility that national rules can provide a corrective to some rather ominous trends that state-by-state actions are adding up to.

QUESTION: What about regional primaries? On the route to a national primary—if one is on that route?

PROFESSOR PRICE: I think that party organizations up and down the line have a tremendous stake in the state-by-state method of delegate selection, and that the decentralization of the process and the kind of role and resources that gives the state organizations is really very important. So I'm very skeptical of any attempt to cluster those contests or to regularize them any further.

At the same time I appreciate the trends that may be pushing us in the direction of further intervention, so I'm really in a quandry as to exactly what the national rules can do and ought to do about some of these trends. Short of truly drastic measures, the potential leverage is very small.

MR. BEVERIDGE: It's occurring bit by bit, anyway. I think you are going to see more of a New England grouping, Massachusetts falling right behind New Hampshire, etc. You may find some natural groupings. I personally think that for the national party to enforce a regional primary would be terribly destructive and that it would be even worse to get the Congress involved. I'm not sure about the legality of Congress becoming involved, but I don't think it is a wise policy.

QUESTION: I would like to return to Jim's question and to your response, Dave, when you mentioned quotas and it really goes back to my original question about the importance of the rules. I think there is a philosophical problem here about how the system is regarded. I think that any set of rules will be arbitrary and what is involved here is a willingness to accept the rules. It's like watching a basketball game or a football game and then in the end saying the outcome wasn't correct, the referees made wrong decisions. I think to appreciate the game you have to be willing to accept a certain amount of arbitrariness and recognize that you can't develop an ideal set of rules. I think that once you go down the path of generating rules that guarantee the fairness of the process and representativeness of the process, inevitably there will be those who come along and say the rules are inadequate, let's change them. So you start out with a few rules and then you expand the list of groups covered by the quotas. It's a problem of such dimension that I don't think you can sort of incapsulate it in the rule-making process of the Democratic party.

It seems that what's really involved here is a lack of faith in the traditional processes of politics. And it's not only within the Democratic party. There is certainly much of that in the Republican party and it's reflected throughout the political process. It's that lack of faith in the process, and I wonder if you could address that?

PROFESSOR PRICE: First of all, the rules are not completely rewritten every four years. I just worked through a rough draft of the North Carolina delegate selection plan for 1984. We are changing what we did in 1980 very little. So it is not as though everything is up for grabs every four years. I think in most states now there is a fairly stable set of procedures in place.

Many people assume that what the national party ought to do, basically, is defer to state organizations. I say at the outset I'm basically sympathetic with that. I think the National Committee often interjects itself in state affairs in an unhelpful way. But I just don't accept the premise that state organizations have a natural health, harmony and productivity about them that places a huge burden of proof on any intrusion.

Let me take the one example of the southern parties. In 1964, as you well know, there were a number of all-white delegations from the southern states. The national Democratic Convention had two percent black delegates. This was in a party which gets thirteen or fifteen percent of its vote nationwide from blacks. There is something on the brink of illegitimacy about such a system—certainly nationally, but even within the states. And sometimes it helps if the state party can get itself off the hook with respect to certain difficult things it needs to do, saying, "These are national standards, national rules and we are part of a national party and we have to abide by these standards." It can help the state deal with racial representation, for example. It makes these questions less divisive and less difficult. It is not clear to me there is an absolute conflict of interest between the state organization and the national rules at that point. I think the national organization, under certain circumstances, can nudge the parties along in productive directions and can in fact make it easier for them to do things, to get over certain difficult decisions, that really will strengthen their hand politically in the end.

Our party in North Carolina is stronger by virtue of the kind of minority participation we have been able to develop, and I have no doubt whatsoever that the national rules helped us get there.

I say this while remaining basically skeptical of this kind of national party role, but I think you have to look at it rule by rule and case by case. I don't think it is self-evident that national intrusion is always destructive of party strength.

MR. BEVERIDGE: If I can interrupt because I've been more skeptical. First of all, you say that all rules are arbitrary. I don't think you can look at these rules and say that all rules are arbitrary. For example, permitting any declared Democrat to participate. I don't think there is anything arbitrary about that. If you can say seventy-five percent have to be elected at a congressional district level and twenty-five percent at large, that's, of course, arbitrary. But there are lots of things in the rules that are not arbitrary. They are usually the rules of more general application: non-discrimination, openness, publicity, and so forth. My criticism is really with the degree of specificity with which the rules are written. I think it is possible to write the rules in a broader, more general way. It may be they are not written that way partially because of history and partially because of lack of trust.

There may be a very positive effect, however, in specific rules—although when I was a student I used to love convention time because of all the fights. But when I grew older and started representing candidates I turned 180 degrees. If you want to be nominated, you want as little deliberation as possible in the convention. Under the old system those fights used to occur on Monday and Tuesday, before the nomination and they were humdingers, whether they were racial exclusion or the famous Eisenhower credentials fight. So that having the delegate selection process follow well defined and logical steps has helped a lot at convention time.

PROFESSOR PRICE: Just briefly, I think in certain areas you are right on target. As someone who has worked with a state party, it seems to me the most destructive set of rules we have is Rule Eleven, the rule dealing with the role of candidate organizations in the process. Most of you are probably roughly familiar with that. But let me just indicate the hammerlock these organizations have on the state parties. That is the real problem, I think, not national intrusion but the shift in the whole delegate selection function to the candidate organizations.

First of all, of course, everyone running for delegate has to declare their presidential preference well in advance and run as someone pledged to a candidate. So far, so good; that seems to be fair enough. That is a kind of truth-in-packaging provision, a reasonable requirement. But that's not enough. We compile a list of everyone running under a candidate's banner and we submit that list to the candidate. The candidate then has to approve it. If he wants to strike a name from the list for any reason whatsoever he can do so. The only requirement is that he leave three names on there for every slot that he's entitled to. Of course it is easy enough if you want—and in some states it has happened—to pad that list so that there are essentially dummy names and you've basically slated your people.

But even *that* is not enough. The candidate comes in with an approved list. Then when you actually pick these delegates— in North Carolina at our district convention, we cannot come into the district convention and elect the delegates we're sending to the national convention. We have to split that district convention into candidate caucuses—because the rule says that at the district level only people who are themselves pledged to a given candidate can vote for "his" delegates. Now that's the one that really sticks in our throat. To come to a district convention, and for that district convention not to be able to vote for the party's representatives at the national convention just sticks in our throat. We devised a system of color-coded ballots so that we didn't actually have to send the Kennedy people into one corner and the Carter people into another. We've tried to minimize the divisive impact. But it is an absurd rule, particularly since these candidates have already been able to veto anyone who was obviously a ringer.

And then of course in 1980, the *coup de grace*, on top of all that, was that if a delegate showed the slightest wavering he could be yanked from the floor of the convention. That, to me, is national rule making at its worst. It is both a cause and a sign of the extent to which this whole process has become a candidate-dominated process.

Now that is what you call really hurting your state organizations, removing the kind of incentives they have to offer their people, removing the role of party leaders in helping send people to the convention. That is really debilitating. In the Hunt Commission—and Hunt wanted this changed, as did many state party leaders—we really fought to loosen Rule 11. What we fought hardest for was to get rid of that requirement that candidate caucuses meet separately at the district level. The Mondale people, the Kennedy people, the labor people dug in and we did not have a chance.

QUESTION: I'd like to comment on a query. In the first place, you seem very aware of the problems created by a rule-making system and yet both of you have commented in a very negative way about the organization which has been created to oversee those rules. You deem that some of the decisions are officious. You are quite troubled, it was suggested, about the staff having the authority to make those kinds of interpretations. Yet I think few scholars who are interested in organization processes themselves would be surprised at all that that kind of organization and authority was created by creating in and of itself a rule-making authority, a rule-making system. So it seems to me that while you are, I think properly, ambivalent about adopting that system, that you shouldn't be surprised or troubled at all by seeing staff in that situation come to have interpretive authority. And if there are mechanisms whereby you can make changes giving greater authority to political figures of the DNC and perhaps elsewhere over those kinds of interpretive decisions, short of changing the rules, I guess I'm a little confused at your apparent ambivalence after once having adopted the system.

MR. BEVERIDGE: Well, if it were a question of surprise, I'm not surprised. I am a Washington lawyer and used to a bureaucracy and arbitrary decision making. If you are saying you are surprised I am involved in the process given my ambivalence about it, I rationalize it in my mind because I think we are trying to establish an attitude which will diminish staff questioning and staff interpretation. We now have as the CRC (Compliance Review Commission) executive director a former state executive leader who was formerly on the receiving end and is very conscious of what you call officious intervention.

As for political leaders, that is not the way it works. Insofar as the official DNC is concerned, they are delighted to have a CRC available. For example, Chuck Mannat will get a telephone call from Jay the governor of Wisconsin about a delegate selection plan. "That is a really creative interesting idea," Mannat will say, "Send it to the CRC." And the CRC gets it, and it's clearly off the wall. Then Mannat can say to the governor, "I thought you really had some creative thought there." The head of the DNC doesn't want to take the responsibility, and certainly nobody from the state congressional delegation wants to take the responsibility. So we are a convenient mechanism. I hope that we can be just that, but in terms of personality we must be less officious, even if we have to carry out some of the dirty work that people want to avoid for strict political reasons. And I personally am enough of a political groupie, that's the way I'm involved.

PROFESSOR PRICE: One of the political accommodations that was made in the last stages of the Hunt Commission's work was to ensure that state party forces would dominate on the Compliance Review Commission. There was a great deal of discontent on the part of state party leaders on the Hunt Commission with the solution that was arrived at on the elected official issue. In the end the elected official group was split between unpledged and pledged delegates, basically because some of the interests on the Commission wanted to keep the number of unpledged delegates down. And so we have two pages of rules where we should have one sentence on this matter of whether party and elected officials are committed or not. There are two separate groups—another absurd rule. In any case, the state party people were very upset over that, and among the accommodations that was worked out was that they would have a very strong hand in the naming of the Compliance Review Commission and staff. So it is a body that is much more oriented toward the state parties than it has probably ever been.

QUESTION: Anne Wexler said as our Commission finished their work that she thought an effort like this would have a long afterlife. Do you think that some of the full consequences of what you did will have an afterlife? And the other part of the question; you said you hadn't talked at all about the Howard Baker problem of helping the full-time legislator in getting better people. Is there anything you would say about that however briefly if you had talked about that?

PROFESSOR PRICE: Well, I haven't thought it through thoroughly, but my basic reaction is that there is very little the rules can do. Because of the cumulative effect of rules, and campaign financing laws, and the media's transformation of the presidential campaign, the kind of presidential nomination system we are working with now is very much tilted against the Baker type of candidate. I think that is unfortunate. I think what the rules can do about it is pretty limited, although it would be worthwhile to give it some thought.

As to the afterlife of what we've done: Despite all the laughing we do about the rules-fetishism of the Democratic party, the situation is not entirely comic. There is a real preoccupation with all this in the party, far too much money and time and energy spent on it. But I do think there is a growing awareness of the problem. I think the present national chairman would like to downplay this kind of activity. He has kept the appointment of new commissions and new rule-making bodies to a minimum. Quantitatively, the Hunt Commission changed the rules less than any other body has. There has been a stabilizing and a settling down of all this. I wouldn't regard it as totally unrealistic to think that rule making might be keyed down even further, and maybe even be left to a DNC subcommittee the next time around.

There are some changes that ought to be made next time around, but if the price of getting those changes was appointing a whole new commission to reopen it all again, I would gladly back off. Still, let me just tick off three or four key areas where it seems to me further changes are desirable. First, as I've indicated, I think this candidate approval apparatus ought to be largely dismantled. I have no illusions about that taking place, though at the margins it might be loosened. One hopeful thing is that none of this is in the charter yet. A lot of the rules have been made permanent party law in the party charter, but the Rule 11 business about the candidates' role is not yet fundamental party law. So there is still a flexibility for change that doesn't exist in other areas. That is a small glimmer of hope, I admit, but there has been some reluctance to give Rule 11 that degree of permanence. In any event, I would place reducing the hammerlock of candidates on the process high on the list.

I think the whole party leader/elected official rule needs to be cleaned up. Get rid of the distinction between pledged and unpledged party leaders and elected officials. Have something like a 25% add-on for unpledged party leaders and elected officials, and let it go at that, which in real percentage terms would be 20% of the national convention.

The equal division and affirmative action programs still pose some problems for the party, but one is reluctant to tamper with something that has achieved a kind of consensus. I think affirmative action for minority groups really works pretty well. Given the range of interests within the party, the present provisions for "goals" for minority groups is something that state parties can work with and can live with. I don't feel the same way about equal division. That is something that, politically, probably will have to be maintained for awhile. But applying equal division to the party leader/elected official group would be a mistake, and that group probably ought to be exempted from the overall calculations. In the long run we need to look at loosening those kinds of constraints.

Finally, front-loading. I have considerable diffidence about plunging in with further rules. I share the presumption against complicating them further and exercising further coercion. However, I feel that this is a serious enough problem to warrent some contraints—at least saying that a state cannot move to a loophole system, a direct-election system, and at the same time move earlier in the process. Some kind of modest scotching of that movement toward the front of the calendar is desirable, even at the price of extending the province of national party rule-making. But I put that forward very tentatively, because I frankly don't have a great deal of confidence in what we could do.

MR. BEVERIDGE: I think that in terms of attracting candidates the financial aspects are much more significant than these rules, and therefore they are marginal in attracting potential government officials. But, the one thing I don't think is touchable in the foreseeable future is equal division. Personally, I think the principle creates extraordinary pressures, but it is now an article of faith in the Democratic party. It is in the Charter. It was remarkable to me when I mentioned what occurred at the last DNC meeting with the so-called Fink Proposal why Democratic heads of state House and Senate wouldn't be automatic selections. The argument immediately raised was, "How many of them are women?" That's all we heard about. The fact is very few are, and that was the strongest argument against it.

PROFESSOR PRICE: That is a very frustrating thing though, because we really tried very hard in the course of the Commission's work to get the state legislators in there to testify and let us know what they wanted. Their organizations didn't even appear, didn't even testify. We could barely get them to focus on the process at all. So at the last minute when Congresswoman Ferraro was putting together the elected official proposal that finally passed, she changed the category from "state legislative leaders" to "state legislators"—very deliberately, to include more women. She consulted with no one from the state legislators' organization, as far as I know, because there was no one to consult with. The state legislators have not involved themselves in the process at all. So it is a little hard to be sympathetic when they come in now and want the matter reopened and the rule rewritten, even though what they are asking for has some merit.

I would agree with you about the political realities on equal division. The reason that this is a more problematic rule than affirmative action is that with affirmative action you are dealing with much smaller percentages. If for some reason at the district level you do not have enough minority delegates selected, then there is always room at the top, in the at-large delegation, to take care of those percentages. There is a kind of norm at work now, a notion of fairness within the state parties, that says you really ought to do that. It is not something people resist or feel resentful about. On the other hand, equal division cannot be handled in that way. There is no way, if you don't have enough women at the district level, to come in at the at-large level and quietly take care of it. You have to impose procedures on your district-level selection process so as to achieve equal division at that level. So that is a very different kind of quota, much more restrictive of the way local and district parties operate.

QUESTION: What percentage of women do you think would be elected as delegates to the Democratic party now if there were no rule?

PROFESSOR PRICE: I think it would be substantial.

MR. BEVERIDGE: If I were to guess—35 or 40.

QUESTION: And then the question I would have is do we really have the problem?

MR. BEVERIDGE: Well you have to ask the women whether there is a problem, don't ask me!

QUESTION: The funny thing about the equal division rule is that it seems to constrain every other choice decision. For example we went to this conference in Wisconsin and started discussing this provision of elected officials, say, 25%. Most of the people at that conference said, "Oh, this elected officials provision is an excellent idea, it gets the party leaders back in."

Almost everyone I think thought it was a good idea. Finally someone said you'll never get 25%, it's impossible. Why? The answer is because most of the elected officials are males and therefore if you add on 25% of elected officials, then you go to the rest of the delegates, the 75%, and most of those you have to force them to be females to end up with an equal division. So it is a clear case in which what seems to be the more important issue has to be dropped and considered in terms of less important.

PROFESSOR PRICE: That is why I say that even if you can't touch equal division in your base delegations, there is a strong case to be made for not applying it to the elected official group, and not requiring the elected official group to be counter-balanced in the regular delegation. We did not do this; politically, it seemed wiser to simply lay peoples' apprehensions to rest and to move on from there. And even so, the "equal power" argument was seriously advanced by some people as a reason for not including the (predominantly male) elected officials at all.

QUESTION: I had a question about your comment that the rules need to be changed because it's too easy for an unknown candidate to get into office and it's too difficult for legislators in Washington to get out and run under these rules. The obvious target of that justification is Jimmy Carter, and there is a judgment there that the administration was bad overall. So one of the things that ought to be changed is the system that got that administration there. But, I think if you go back over the last two elections conducted under the rules the theory of the legislator having trouble running isn't really carried through. In 1976 if you take Martin Schram's argument about the campaign, it was less a product of the rules than a product of the fact that Jimmy Carter didn't make mistakes that others made under those rules. Morris Udall was a very strong candidate in the beginning and was running very successfully under the rules. In 1980, one prominent legislator made it very difficult for an incumbent president, and eventually at the convention had significant say over the platform and over Democratic party finances. And now in 1984, three of the four declared candidates are legislators. So my question I guess is, again, is it necessary to focus on the rules, or are we just building up a construct here to go against the Carter administration and some other things, the Washington anti-establishment thing.

PROFESSOR PRICE: Well, I didn't mean to imply a

thorough-going critique of the Carter administration in the off-hand comment I made. Nor would one want to argue that the rules have absolutely predisposed the system in one direction or the other. All that was said was that there is a tendency in the rules to give certain advantages to people who are not employed, not just to people who don't have legislative duties, but to people in general who have the time and resources to spend endless hours in living rooms.

I think the Kennedy case could cut both ways. Another question is what kind of challenge to an incumbent this system makes possible, and maybe even likely. The Reagan insurgency in 1976 and the Kennedy insurgency in 1980 were far more likely under the present rules than they would have been previously. So it's a question of opening up the process in a way that puts a premium on a certain intense kind of personal campaign two years in advance that almost guarantees challenges for sitting Presidents.

Yes, we've opened up the process, we've opened it up with a vengeance. And while a certain amount of openness, a certain possibility of challenge, is desirable, I think there are serious questions as to whether we have not gone too far in that direction. That is what people who have been involved in rethinking the rules have considered. Not that you ought to put New Hampshire and Iowa out of business entirely, but that you certainly ought to give more weight to the mainline industrial states that are the party's central constituency; give more weight to the judgments of party and elected officials. Of course, other things being equal, that would reduce the possibilities of an insurgent candidacy or of an unknown getting in. It doesn't completely shut it down but it reduces the chance. That is a judgment that we make with our eyes open. We think that it is the direction we ought to take.

MR. BEVERIDGE: And there is another important factor, I think, that was very clearly aimed at the Carter administration. There was a perception that once President Carter was elected there was a problem of governance. There was the strong feeling that in the course of the nominating process a candidate should be forced to meet with and engage in some dialogue with elected officials, especially at the national level of the House and Senate. Because if you are elected, you are going to have to deal with them and I think there was a very strong feeling that Carter had not had that experience, and that his administration would have been much better for having established those contacts before his election. So I personally think the unpledged elected official provision has a lot more to do with governance than with the process of nomination.

QUESTION: You had said that you thought that the provision for the selection of the House and Senate members as convention delegates is a transitional measure. What did you mean?

PROFESSOR PRICE: I'm uncertain about that. I said *possibly* it was a transitional measure. I think it is viewed very widely as an experiment. A number of people who supported it did so because they thought it was the most promising way to get congressmen involved in the process in short order. There was—one must confess—also some uncertainty about the state organizations and whether they would actually pick these people. There was some fear that some state organizations might be so much under the control of different constituency groups and so forth that they might not even send the party's main elected officials. But basically, the decision didn't derive from any very sophisticated thinking about the state party's role or that sort of thing. It was more of a pragmatic effort to get these people there and also to accommodate the strong interest of the congressional leadership in experimenting with this kind of role. I don't think there is a lot of firm conviction behind it, that this is the way to do it from now on. I think it will be up for re-examination and may be changed four or eight years from now.

In the long run, I would favor moving to a system where the state party names all its people and the congressional caucus is not involved. But it struck me as a perfectly reasonable short-term experiment.

QUESTION: Well, I think the question I have is kind of broad maybe you could speak to it briefly. You seem to suggest that any future changes made in the rules will likely shift from a new commission to maybe a DNC subcommittee. Is that likely to decrease the influence of candidate organizations?

PROFESSOR PRICE: Well, I should say that I don't really say that as a prediction. I think it is feasible and I think it is desirable.

MR. BEVERIDGE: I think it would if you had an ongoing subcommittee. One of the problems about the Hunt Commission or any commission which is highly focused and has to be balanced in all respects, is that it is an easier forum for candidates and potential candidates to play upon then an ongoing subcommittee of the DNC.

QUESTION: And would it increase the power of the state organization?

PROFESSOR PRICE: Yes. A DNC group could be counted on, I think, to represent state party interests more strongly. I do not think a DNC group would be any less responsive to the different demographic constituencies. A DNC group would be just as constrained in terms of affirmative action and equal division as the commission was. Potentially, though, they might be much more sympathetic toward loosening some of that Rule 11 apparatus with respect to candidate control of the process.

QUESTION: The DNC group would not be likely to make major changes either to increase the rule stringency or to dismantle the rules?

PROFESSOR PRICE: Depending on how it was chosen, of course, I would expect the center of gravity on a representative DNC committee to be in the direction that the Hunt Commission took, only more so. And I think you would have more interest in a role for the state organizations, that you would have a greater possibility of loosening some of the candidate control. The state parties were represented on the Hunt Commission, but not nearly in proportion to the number of seats they have on the DNC. At most I would guess twenty percent of the commission had primarily state party affiliations; on the DNC it would be more like 40 percent.

MR. THOMPSON: We wish to thank you for a wonderfully informative discussion of the presidential nominating process. You have viewed the process from two quite different perspectives but your insights and judgments have converged. Together you have given us a complete picture of the problem as we have received from any source.

Footnotes

1. Cite Bibby *et al*, article in May, 1983 *American Journal of Political Science.*

2. Charles O. Jones, *The Minority Party in Congress.* (Boston: Little, Brown, 1970).

3. In Joseph Califano, *Presidential Nation.* (New York:W. W. Norton, 1975), ch. 7.

4. Nelson Polsby, *Consequences of Party Reform.* (New York: Oxford University Press, 1983), ch. 3.

5. See *Commonsense*, vol. 4, no. 2 (1981); and vol. 5, no. 1 (1982).

6. *Washington Post*, November 14, 1981, p. 23.

MONEY AND THE PRESIDENTIAL NOMINATING PROCESS

Herbert Alexander

NARRATOR: We're pleased to welcome you to a Forum with Herb Alexander. Over the years he has been Mr. Money and Politics and those of us who have followed the subject have come to respect and recognize the contribution that he has made through steady and consistent pursuit of this interest. He received his M.A. from the University of Connecticut, his Ph.D. from Yale University. He began his study of the financing of campaigns and elections as part of a research project at the University of North Carolina at Chapel Hill headed by Alex Heard. Heard went on to become chancellor at Vanderbilt University and chairman of the board of the Ford Foundation. He is recently retired and is himself heading up a project on presidential nominations.

Herb Alexander's lasting achievement is his role as director of the Citizen's Research Foundation, established in Princeton in 1958 and continuing into the present. He's been a professor of political science at the University of Southern California since 1978, he's held a whole series of advisory and administrative positions having to do with the financing of campaigns. He's been executive director of the President's Committee on Campaign Costs, in the early 1960s; he was consultant on presidential campaign activities to the President, to the House Administration Committee, comptroller general, and to the Senate Select Committee on Presidential Campaign Activities. In short, he's been much in demand as the political scientist who knew most about money and politics. He's the author of numerous studies including a multi-volume study of money and politics, a book on the financing of the 1972 campaign and another on the financing of the 1976 election, a book called *Financing Politics*, and many other articles and monographs on this subject. It is our privilege to have him speak on the regulation and funding of presidential elections.

MR. ALEXANDER: Thank you very much. I'm happy to be here at the Center and at the University. I have been here a number of times before and I'm always pleased to be in Charlottesville.

I think that it's clear that electoral politics has been undergoing changes of immense proportions with the advent of professionalism in politics, the application of high technology to politics. The costs of politics have soared with public opinion polling, with computer usage both for strategy and for direct mail, and with the use of electronics including of course television which is very costly particularly in presidential campaigns. But campaigning for President has changed even more than campaigning for other offices. And the reason is of course that over the past decade or more there have been a number of changes in the ways in which delegates have been selected in the nomination phase of the presidential selection process. But in addition, starting in the 1976 presidential elections, and including the 1980 presidential elections, under the Federal Election Campaign Act there has been a system of public funding of presidential elections. Now that system of public funding has had impact and has affected the ways in which the campaigns for nomination and for election have been run.

I think that it might be desirable to talk just a bit about the ways in which the public funding system operates. In the Federal Election Campaign Act of 1971 and again in 1974 there are provisions for public funding of presidential campaigns ultimately in three phases, in the pre-nomination campaigns, funding for the parties in their arrangements for holding the national nominating conventions and then in the post-nomination phase for the general election period. As you well know, the money for public funds comes from the tax check off and each of you has the opportunity to check off one dollar or two on a joint return for a presidential election campaign fund. That is collected on an annual basis. The money is aggregated and the payout is made in the presidential election year.

In the pre-nomination period, candidates can qualify for public funds by receiving five thousand dollars in contributions up to two hundred fifty dollars each in twenty states. It's not a particularly difficult matter for most candidates to qualify for the public funds. And in fact there have been some unusual candidates who have been able to do so. In 1976 Ellen McCormack ran as a Democrat on the right to life platform and was able to qualify for public funds; in 1980, Lyndon LaRouche, who heads a party called the U.S. Labor party but nevertheless ran as a Democrat, was able to qualify for public funds. Of course major candidates whom you read about are also able to do so simply by arranging networks of fundraising activities in twenty states submitting the names of the individual contributors to the Federal Election Commission and qualifying for matching funds. The federal government matches each contribution made by an individual up to two hundred fifty dollars.

In the financing for the national nominating conventions the major parties receive funding based on a formula of three million dollars plus a cost-of-living adjustment every four years. In 1980 the Democratic party and the Republican party nationally received $4.4 million to run their national nominating conventions.

Once the candidates are nominated the public funding system provides flat grants. Also based on the formula, the basic amount of public funding is $20 million, adjusted every four years for cost of living increases. In 1980 in the prenomination campaigns candidates could spend up to $14 million and receive half of that in matching funds. In the general election flat grants are made to the major party candidates. The amount that was made available to Mr. Reagan and to Mr. Carter in 1980 was $29.4 million in flat grants. In that general election period candidates for President who are accepting the public funds cannot raise money privately. In the general election if they accept the flat grants, they cannot accept private money in any way, shape, or form. However the national party can spend money according to a formula on behalf of the presidential ticket and in 1980 that amount was $4.6 million, with the result that the amount of money in control of the candidates Carter and Reagan in 1980 was $34 million each.

I would like to talk about the general election first, because I think we can talk about it more quickly than the prenomination period where there is more controversy. The 1980 campaigns for President I found to be very interesting and in fact exciting because as the law developed and as litigation was pursued, as there were court cases dealing with public funding and other aspects of funding for presidential campaigns among other campaigns, there developed in the general election a really unique situation in which there are three parallel campaigns for President.

On the one hand, in the first campaign the presidential candidate controls the money which is the flat grant plus the money that is spent on behalf of the ticket by the national committee—$34 million in 1980. There is a second parallel campaign which is sanctioned by law in which there can be spending on behalf of the ticket in coordinated expenditures. The coordinated expenditures can be spent by state and local party committees in which they can spend unlimited amounts of money on behalf of the presidential ticket so long as the money is not spent on media but is spent on volunteer activity. That means that state and local party committees can spend unlimited amounts of money on registration campaigns, get out the vote campaigns, door to door canvassing, phone banks— whatever is not direct advertising. The prerogative for direct advertising remains with the presidential campaign and its central headquarters. And so in 1980 there was more evidence of activity by state and local parties and there came to be developed the concept of "soft money" going into the presidential campaigns.

Some of you may have read two articles by Elizabeth Drew in *New Yorker* Magazine in which she explored in one of those articles the concept of "soft money" and found that in some states, contrary to federal law, corporate money, labor union money was going directly into the presidential campaigns through the vehicle of contributions to state and local party committees. She used a figure of $9 million from the parties on the Republican side but my figure is higher. In my book, *Financing the 1980 Election*, I found $15 million had filtered through the Republican party committees and had been spent on behalf of the presidential ticket in coordinated expenditures. The Democrats raised about $4 million for these purposes. Some of the money is legal under federal law, some of it is illegal under federal law, but nevertheless all of it is acceptable because state law governs the raising of that money for use by state and local party committees. And of course some states permit corporate contributions and union contributions. Federal law does not permit labor or corporate contributions. And so in that second campaign we're finding a mixture of federally governed money as well as money from the private sector that is governed by either federal or state law.

Also in the area of the second parallel campaign is an element of coordinated expenditures that are, for example, expenditures by labor unions on behalf of endorsed candidates. The Carter/Mondale ticket in the general election period in 1980 benefited from about $15 million spent by the labor organizations in coordinated expenditures with the national Democratic ticket. There were a few other kinds of minimal expenditures in the second campaign.

Then there is a third parallel campaign sanctioned by federal law and sanctioned by the courts now. The United States Supreme Court in the case of *Buckley v. Valeo* in 1976 said that independent expenditures could not be limited so long as they were spent out of pocket by individuals and by interest groups in ways that were not coordinated with the candidate or his campaign. And so you recall the expenditures that were made on behalf of Reagan in the prenomination period by organizations such as National Conservative Political Action Committee (NCPAC), Fund for a Conservative Majority, and other organizations that could independently spend money on behalf of Reagan in the prenomination period or then again in the general election on behalf of the Reagan/Bush ticket. Those expenditures in the general election period amounted to in excess of $10 million.

And so if you conceptualize with me these three parallel campaigns it's a curious mixture of federal law, state law, candidate control, limits, coordinated expenditures, and unlimited independent expenditures. And if you find it hard to follow you should try to teach this to undergraduates. In any case, the fact is that the Federal Election Campaign Act is very complex. Now of course there are efforts to extend public funding to senatorial and congressional campaigns. And I don't think they're going to be successful in the near future. But in any case the impact would be much greater because we would be dealing with many more hundreds of campaigns than we are when there is only public funding in presidential campaigns.

In presidential campaigns, of course, the number of candidates qualifying for matching funds, for example in 1976, was fifteen candidates. In 1980 it was ten candidates receiving matching funds in their efforts to raise money and to qualify for matching funds in their prenomination campaigns. So far in the 1984 campaigns for nomination there are seven announced candidates on the Democratic side, no announced candidates on the Republican side, and I think four candidates have already qualified for matching funds based on fundraising they have already done in 1982 or 1983. But they will not receive payouts in matching funds until the election year. There will be a large infusion of money in early January for the Mondale campaign, the Glenn campaign, the Cranston campaign, and the Hart campaign. In fact it's a very interesting phenomenon that, as discussed among knowledgeable people, the Cranston campaign and the Hart campaign are in financial difficulty, are not going to go anywhere, but the candidates cannot afford to quit. They cannot afford to get out because they have debts and they are waiting until January to get matching funds for a new infusion of money that will enable them to pay off their debts and perhaps to compete in the early primaries and caucuses.

In 1984, interestingly, because the Democratic rules were changed there is going to be a very heavy concentration of primaries and caucuses in a three-week period. Just to backtrack a little, in 1980 and also in 1976 there were five weeks between the Iowa caucuses and the New Hampshire primary and then there were two weeks between the New Hampshire primary and the deluge of other primaries and caucuses. The Democrats formed a Hunt Commission which made recommendations to close the window, that is to try to concentrate primaries and caucuses within a more inclusive period of time, again giving Iowa and New Hampshire their historical and traditional prerogative of going to the polls a week before anybody else in the country. Of course that's a whole different subject but Iowa and New Hampshire are hardly representative of America, they do not have large cities, do not have large minority groups and the result is in the past a candidate who won the Iowa caucuses and the New Hampshire primary and then got his picture on the cover of *Time* and *Newsweek* with media hype was possibly on the road to getting the nomination.

In any case, the Hunt Commission made recommendations for change in 1984, to collapse the period. In addition there are some states which are changing from primaries to caucuses. Given the period of Iowa one week, of New Hampshire the next week, and then a series of thirteen more caucuses and primaries within a ten-day period means that that concentration is putting tremendous pressure on the candidates and I think giving a real advantage to candidates who are the front runners or candidates who have large bank accounts and who are going to be able to spend their money in these various primary and caucus states in concentrated ways. One of the advantages in earlier times, was that if a candidate did well in Iowa he could exploit that showing, raise money, additional money that then would enable him to move step by step, primary by caucus, and then win New Hampshire and then raise more money. But now there is such a concentration in that three-week period that the candidates really won't have opportunity to exploit a good showing in Iowa and New Hampshire in order to survive the test of the other primaries. That is one of the reasons that candidates for 1984 got a very early start.

The Federal Election Campaign Act imposed contribution limits as you well know, no more than a thousand dollars for an individual per candidate per election, which means that candidates have had to seek new financial sources in order to raise funds. That thousand dollar contribution limit went into effect January 1, 1975 and if the value of the dollar is held constant a thousand dollar contribution then would be worth about $500 today. At the same time the amounts of money that the candidates can legitimately spend under the expenditure limits has increased according to cost of living adjustments. Now public funding has also increased according to the expenditure limits. But nevertheless the candidates need to find more and more contributors in order to raise for 1984, for example, what would be the expenditure limit—$19 million as compared with $11 million in 1976 in the prenomination period.

And so we have the disparity between the rising expenditure limits, and of course commensurate with the rising expenditure limits has come the opportunity, if you can call it that, to participate in more primaries and caucuses because the number of primaries has increased from many fewer to thirty or more. The number will be decreasing for 1984, although there will be more caucuses. Picking up some of that slack that may not be spent on primary elections in the state, because caucuses can be less expensive than open primaries, has been the devices that have developed in terms of straw polls, cattle shows, forums—you know, in which all the candidates are asked to come to an event and to give a speech and to show themselves off in sort of a cattle auction. There's of course a good deal of media hype concentrating on these early events which are taking place now, and in fact today there is one in Maine.

And so the candidates are spending in these events and are stretching their budgets because of the difficulty of raising money and because of the increased demand for participation in the events including primaries and caucuses. Because of the concentration of primaries and caucuses I think that the demand for money has been insatiable and people draw conclusions when candidates need money. They might undertake obligations that they might otherwise not. I don't think that applies as much to presidential candidates as to candidates in the Senate and House and other offices but the fact is that the financial pressures are immense to raise the necessary dollars in this prenomination period.

I left out the fact that in the prenomination period there are also state limits on the amounts the candidates can spend. In other words there are limitations on the amounts that candidates can spend in Virginia seeking delegates or in New Hampshire or Iowa or California or New York seeking delegates. The Federal Election Commission has given a preliminary listing for 1984 of expenditures which the candidates can undertake seeking delegates. In Virginia for example the amount will be about $1.3 million. Now if you added each of the fifty states it would come to much more than the nineteen million dollars that the candidates will be able to spend seeking nomination. What that means is that the candidates have to pick and choose in their spending. They can't participate to the full extent by spending to the limit in each of the fifty states. That usually isn't necessary because past experience has been that the candidates have been chosen pretty early on, in effect by the combination of good showings in Iowa and New Hampshire, the media hype, and then a few subsequent primaries in which enough delegates are secured to enable the candidates to get nominated at the convention.

Very curious activities have had to be undertaken in order for candidates to survive. There has been tremendous impact of the expenditure limits at the state level in particular so that the candidates have had to indulge in cash management and encounter cash flow problems in ways that previous candidates never did. The law has simply forced candidates to be very careful in spending their money and in allocating it from state to state, making investments, making decisions about whether to go to the limit in one state and not spend money in another state. And so questions of strategy and tactics have derived from these expenditure limits apart from the ability of the candidates to raise the money.

Very curious things also happen with respect to the state expenditure limitation. In New Hampshire, for example, in

1980 the expenditure limit was $294,000 that Carter and Kennedy and whoever was running could spend. Two hundred ninety-four thousand dollars is not a lot of money even in a small state such as New Hampshire when so much rides on "winning" that state in the polling that takes place on election day. And so subterfuges have developed in which the candidates campaign during the day in New Hampshire but stay with their entourages in Boston or in Vermont overnight so that the costs then get ascribed to Vermont or Massachusetts and they don't have to therefore apply all the costs and go over the expenditure limits in New Hampshire. Americans are very clever and resourceful but I think that it gives some indication of the difficulty with expenditure limits in the American system, which is pluralistic and which there are some many openings for disbursement.

Add to that situation what happened in 1980, which was that the groups such as NCPAC and the Fund for Conservative Majority spent literally scores of thousands of dollars on behalf of Reagan in independent expenditures, not associated with the Reagan campaign so that Reagan had a real advantage in that money was being spent on his behalf. He could not control it and when you can't control it it might be counterproductive. But nevertheless it was being spent on his behalf in those states—in some of the early states. And in fact in the North Carolina primary Jesse Helms' Congressional Club spent considerable money on behalf of Reagan. In Texas the Fund for the Conservative Majority spent money on behalf of Reagan. And the result was that that third parallel campaign was operating independently of the other two campaigns but nevertheless having an impact and possibly a counterproductive impact. Given all those factors, it's very interesting to speculate about what could happen in 1984 for example should President Reagan decide not to run. There are some people in Washington that still think he might not run but it would cause some havoc in the Republican party. There would be a sudden scrambling for money to establish organizations in order to compete for that nomination among at least four candidates—presumably Bush, Baker, Dole, and Kemp.

The fact is that the Federal Election Campaign Act has rigidified the system to a great extent. If you think back to 1968, when in late February Bobby Kennedy decided to run and in eleven weeks before his assassination spent eleven million dollars—he spent a million dollars a week in his campaign for nomination in 1968. In 1980 Jerry Ford considered the possibility of becoming a candidate in March, and had he done so, even with his potential fundraising ability, he would have had a very difficult time raising large amounts of money in that remaining period before the convention. Jerry Ford did not run not because of the financial considerations so much as because too many delegates had already been pledged prior to the time he considered getting into the fray. But the fact is that the Federal Election Campaign Act has rigidified the system. We don't have quite the same spontaneity and flexibility that occurred previously when a candidate like Kennedy could suddenly jump in at a time when there were no contribution limits and he could raise hundreds of thousands of dollars from single individuals, and did so. Kennedy had several contributors of $500,000 to his campaign in 1968. You can't do things like that today. By instituting the contribution limits the Congress imposed the concept of broadening financial bases and constituencies. But the candidates have a very hard time in raising the requisite dollars in order to compete effectively.

QUESTION: You didn't say anything about minor parties and how they are financed.

MR. ALEXANDER: I didn't, but I'll be glad to. Under the Federal Election Campaign Act a major party is defined as one which received twenty-five percent of the vote in the previous election. That immediately qualifies the Republicans and the Democrats for public funding in the conventions and in the general election period. The act also defines a minor party as one in which the party received five percent or more of the vote four years before. And no candidate of a minor party has qualified because minor parties are not in the habit of getting as much as five percent of the vote. However, there is another provision of the law which enables a minor party to receive money retroactively if in the current election it receives five percent of the vote or more.

That was the situation in which John Anderson contested in 1980 as an independent candidate—mind you, not as a minor party candidate but as an independent candidate—and he made application to the Federal Election Commission to be considered for post-election funding if he got five percent of the vote. As it turned out he received 6.5 percent of the vote and so the Federal Election Commission recognized him as the functional equivalent of a minor party and provided 4.2 million dollars of funding to his campaign after the election. Now there is also a provision of the law which says that a candidate or a party which receives funding then will receive it four years hence. And so John Anderson presumably will be eligible for funding in 1984 based on his 1980 performance. However, the Federal Election Commission has to certify that the new party which John Anderson appears to be forming is the same party as the one that he ran under as an independent candidate in 1980 and that will probably occur.

But in any case that provision puts a minor party candidate or an independent candidate at a disadvantage, because, you see, from the time that Carter and Reagan were nominated they did not have to do any fundraising. They got their flat grants, $29.4 million. John Anderson had to be raising money at the same time that he was campaigning and competing against Carter and Reagan and so that immediately put him at a disadvantage because the largest contribution he could receive was a thousand dollars. In fact, Anderson undertook a program of loans and then used the $4.2 million to pay them back when he got the money retroactively after qualifying for the public fund. So that is one disadvantage which the minor party candidate or independent candidate functions under.

But even looking at the laws that exist, the question is whether in 1984 there will be the same demand for John Anderson that there was in 1980. And if you look at the history of minor parties in this country it is not very satisfactory in terms of their coming back four years later, so there's been some criticism even of that provision for funding four years later because what it does is it gives grounds for a person like Anderson to form a party and to be into the fray four years later when it is questionable whether he would have under other circumstances had survived to try another round. If you look at the Progressives, the Bullmoosers, the 1948 parties, the Dixicrats and the Progressives, the George Wallace candidacy—four years later none of them came back. And so what the law is doing is almost ensuring that they will be back four years later once they qualify.

QUESTION: Hiring them to run.

MR. ALEXANDER: Yes. But on the other hand it is a disadvantage for a candidate in those circumstances. The formula by which Anderson got $4.2 million is based on his proportion of the vote as compared with the average of the proportion that the major party candidates receive.

QUESTION: When Cronkite interviewed Kennedy right

after the Oregon victory I think Cronkite chided him about spending so much money and Kennedy's response was, "Well, if you media people would give us 'free time' we could solve this whole problem." Wishful thinking. Is there any possibility that this can occur?

MR. ALEXANDER: Well, if it were to occur I think it would be much easier to legislate in presidential campaigns than in Senate and House campaigns. Political broadcasting is a very tough subject. The notion of requiring broadcasters to provide time as a condition of licensing is one that has been around for a long time. You get into a lot of difficulties because audience ranges don't coincide with political jurisdictions. For example in New York City, New York City channels cover parts of Connecticut and New Jersey and there are forty-two congressional districts covered within that range. So if you get into senatorial and congressional campaigns it is a lot harder. If you are talking about presidential, it's much easier because you are talking about all fifty states regardless, except of course in the prenomination period where a candidate is campaigning in the Massachusetts primary or the South Carolina primary. But in any case section 315—which is misnamed "equal time provision," it's actually "equal opportunity provision" and time is not necessarily the same as opportunity—states that if a station provides time to one candidate for office it has to provide equal opportunity for similar time for other candidates. Same if it sells time. It has to provide opportunity for other candidates to buy time in that time period. But the presidential campaigns are much easier to deal with than others. The League of Women Voters staged a debate in 1980 and also in 1976 and the networks covered those debates so there was some free time.

In addition the broadcast provisions have been relaxed to some extent over the past couple of decades because of exemptions, which are called "news exemptions," for on-the-spot coverage, for interview programs, and the rest.

If you're thinking of the networks just providing time for the candidates to use in their own ways, I don't think that's very likely in the American system. In the British system, in other mature democracies particularly where there is a BBC type organization, time is provided free and candidates cannot purchase time. But comparisons are hazardous because in those parliamentary systems the time goes to the parties, not to the candidates. We live in a candidate-centered culture. It is very difficult to give time to the Democratic party or to the Republican party if you're talking about more than just the presidential campaigns. And so those are not necessarily great models for use in the American system where the emphasis is on the candidate rather than on the party and where the candidate may well campaign apart from the party and not want to be labeled a Republican or Democrat.

QUESTION: You were talking about the second parallel campaign and you mention among other things that those coordinated expenditures would include, for example, some contributions by the AFL-CIO to the Democratic party candidates. Would that not be true for any PAC group? Any PAC group could be involved in doing the same thing and at the same time be involved in making other independent expenditures.

MR. ALEXANDER: That's right. But the business community has not been as involved in campaign activities of the type that the labor unions have been involved in—having joint rallies with candidates, registration and get-out-to-vote campaigns, phone banks, and things of that nature for which labor has had reservoirs of person power. It has had the ability to generate people to do things like that. The corporate PACs, the association PACs, are not as involved in that kind of activity, although they raise more money and spend more money than labor PACs. Their focus has largely been on congressional campaigns and not on presidential. PAC money to presidential campaigns is rather minimal. About one percent of the money that was raised by all the Democratic and Republican candidates running seeking nomination in 1980 came from PACs.

QUESTION: Is there an unlimited amount of money coming in from the check off or is the Election Commission having to be careful about how it divides?

MR. ALEXANDER: The check off rates over the past five years have been fairly stable although this past year the rate has been down. But the rate has been between twenty-five and twenty-nine percent of individual taxpayers who check off. And of course if people are married they can check off two dollars instead of one. The rate has been between twenty-five and twenty-nine percent consistently. The money is raised on an annual basis and accrued over a four year period with the payout made in the election year. The amounts of money available have been greater than the amounts paid out. However, there will come a time when there may be pressure on the system simply because the expenditure limits are being raised and as the expenditure limits are being raised according to increases in the consumer price index, more money is being spent in the system each year. For example in 1976 about $70 million was spent in those three phases. In 1980 it was $100 million. In 1984 it may be $130 to $150 million that is paid out. It may be less than that proportionate raise because there may not be competition in the Republican party. If Reagan runs and there's no competition, that means that Bush isn't out raising money and getting matching funds and Baker and the other candidates as well. So there may be less pressure in 1984 because the only contest would be on the Democratic side in that prenomination period. But in any case there have been surpluses after 1976; after 1980 there was a surplus of almost $80 million. If that money is invested the profit accrues to the Treasury Department and not to the fund.

QUESTION: Mr. Alexander, in the third phase that you mentioned I think you referred to the fact that under the Buckley case the contributions to that were without limitations.

MR. ALEXANDER: I didn't say the contributions could be unlimited. What I said was that expenditures could be unlimited, that is, out of pocket expenditures. You can buy an ad in the newspaper, you can buy posters, you can buy pins out of your own pocket, you can seek to buy television time, but you can't make contributions in excess of five thousand dollars to an organization which is engaging in independent expenditures. So it has to be out of pocket expenses.

QUESTION: Ok, I'll change the word then from contributions to expenditures. This on the Buckley case. I'm wondering whether or not that is constitutionally based because given the current information concerning individual wealth that goes into sometimes multi-billions of dollars, one can conceive of a wide open field for expenditures that are non-directed. But if one, two, or more people wish to undertake such a campaign it could be the introduction of a force that has never been exploited before. Is this a possibility?

MR. ALEXANDER: Well, first of all you're absolutely right. There are concentrations of wealth and in 1980 one Houston entrepreneur spent $600,000 out of his own pocket on behalf first of John Connally and then of Reagan. There were a couple of others who spent $100,000. Norman Lear spent $100,000 on behalf of John Anderson, Stewart Mott spent $100,000 on behalf of Kennedy and Anderson, and in addition there are organizations such as NCPAC which were engaging in independent expenditures. But if NCPAC came to you for a contribution the most you could give to NCPAC would be $5,000—you can give $5,000 to NCPAC because it's a multi-candidate committee.

QUESTION: I can understand the restriction on gifts. I was probing for the philosophical base of the Court decision.

MR. ALEXANDER: Well, the Supreme Court has maintained with respect to independent expenditures that there is constitutional interest in robust discussion and dialogue without limitations so long as that money is spent uncoordinated. You know the concept really is that people should be able to write a leaflet, stand on a street corner, and pass it out. The concept is that people ought to be able to put up lawn signs that say "I'm for Reagan," "I'm for Carter"—whatever. That concept is what led the Supreme Court to say we cannot limit expenditures. Now there are some problems with that in that the Supreme Court was not as clear about groups as it was about individuals. But by inference, groups can spend unlimited amounts. I should say that the Congress intended that there be limitations on independent expenditures and in the 1974 law put a limitation of $1,000 on these independent expenditures out of pocket. And when the Buckley case was brought, the Supreme Court faced thirty-four different constitutional issues related to this law, and found in the case of independent expenditures that limitations were unconstitutional.

However there is another provision of the iaw which you may be reading about. After the Buckley case the Congress rewrote portions of the law to conform it to the doctrine of the Supreme Court but failed to change one provision of the Presidential Campaign Funding Act which does set a limit on $1,000 on independent expenditures in publicly funded campaigns for President. The Federal Election Commission is trying to enforce that and right now is in the courts with NCPAC over that because NCPAC wants to spend more than a thousand dollars on behalf of Reagan in 1984, at least it did prior to the shooting down of the Korean airliner. NCPAC isn't so sure it is friendly to Reagan now.

But in any case there is litigation in progress about that section but I think that the courts will uphold the right of groups as well as individuals to spend unlimited amounts of money. And it's in the nature of constitutional provisions that really deal not just with freedom of speech and not just with concepts of robust discussion but also deal with the right of association, the right of like-minded people to get together and form a political committee to achieve certain political goals. And so I think that you have that combination of freedom of speech and freedom of association which raises questions about how well you can regulate independent expenditures, if at all, and how well you can regulate political action committees, because political action committees are essentially groups of like-minded people gathered together to achieve certain political goals.

Now the Federal Election Commission has written regulations which deal with independent expenditures and there are certain things which you cannot do. For example, Stewart Mott, who is a General Motors heir as you may well know, and who is a liberal spender as well as a liberal, asked the Federal Election Commission for a ruling in which he said: I want to spend money on behalf of John Anderson and Norman Lear out in Los Angeles wants to spend money on behalf of John Anderson. Why can't we pool our efforts? And so if the bill comes to $100,000, he'll pay $50,000 and I'll pay $50,000. The Federal Election Commission said you cannot do that. The act of two people coming together forms a political committee. And then the law becomes operative and you are limited to a $1,000 contribution if it's for a single candidate, $5,000 if it's a multi-candidate committee operating on behalf of five or more candidates. So the Federal Election Commission has sought to refine and define what an independent expenditure is.

But political actors are resourceful and ingenious. Terry Dolan has been one of the most resourceful and ingenious and has found ways of dealing with these kinds of restrictions. For example, one of the regulations of the Federal Election Commission says that for independent expenditures you cannot go to the candidates and coordinate spending with them. What Terry Dolan did was ingenious. He and NCPAC went to the Utah Republican convention with his own camera crew and filmed Reagan at the rostrum and used excerpts of that in spot announcements that looked as if they had been staged by Reagan himself. But it was an independent expenditure because Reagan had not cooperated. The camera crew was simply there and pictured him saying this was his position on social security or whatever. And so there is ingenuity and resourcefulness right along the line.

I think that when you come to questions of regulations of money you really have to recognize the pluralistic nature of American politics, the difficulty of putting a restriction here which then finds money carving new channels and popping up there, and the various ways in which if you put limits here issues suddenly become important and a whole new area of expenditure takes place—right to life or whatever. And the result is that in some ways it's just extremely frustrating to try to regulate this area because there are so many areas where there are openings for disbursement in related ways that can be helpful. I indicated that some of those independent expenditures might be counterproductive. I mean the KKK could come in and start spending money on behalf of a candidate. That might be harmful and very counterproductive but there is nothing that the candidate can do to control that expenditure and so we're caught up in a system that is very free-wheeling, that is very open, and raises real questions about strict limitations.

Now I've personally been in favor of contribution limits. I personally think that disclosure is essential. We now have very good disclosure. The contribution limit for individuals of $1,000 is much too low. I would like to raise the contribution limit for individuals to $5,000, the same as for political action committees. I have been in favor of partial public funding. I like the matching grant system much more than the flat grant system in the general election. But I have never been convinced that expenditure limits are desirable because they give the illusion of controlling money when they really don't, because there are these other parallel things going on in which money is being spent on behalf of the candidate. There are some political scientists who subscribe to the view of floors without ceilings. And I'm one of them. I think that you can conceptualize public funding as a floor giving candidates money that enabled them at least minimal access to the electorate. Beyond that if they can raise money and spend it, I think they should be able to. It's a nice little phrase—floors without ceilings—because I think that the history is that ceilings are not going to be workable. They give the illusion of limiting without really doing so. Particularly when you get Supreme Court decisions such as the *Buckley* case on independent expenditures, what you are doing is when you limit expenditures you are triggering these other kinds of activities that are not accountable in the same way as if the money is in the hands and control of the candidate.

Now I happen to believe that not all of the people but some of the people who contributed to NCPAC for independent expenditures would have preferred to give the money to Reagan directly. But they couldn't do it because either they have reached their limit in the prenomination period, they gave $1,000 and that was it, or else in the general election period they couldn't contribute at all except to the Republican National Committee which was spending money on behalf of the Reagan ticket. But they couldn't give directly to Reagan in the general election period and so I think that the system would be better, more accountable, if the candidate at least controlled the money. But as long as we subscribe to the notion that there are going to be expenditure limits in this tightly and rigidly controlled campaign, other people are going to find other ways to filter money into the system and I would prefer accountable money than nonaccountable money.

NCPAC money—I only use NCPAC in the illustrative sense because they've been in the forefront of independent expenditures but there are other organizations doing it as well—NCPAC money is really not accountable. That was clear in Maryland in the NCPAC attacks on Senator Sarbanes, not a presidential campaign. NCPAC went in very early against Sarbanes before the Republicans had even nominated a candidate to run against him, went in a year or more before. They actually did Sarbanes a good turn because they energized his campaign early. They really wanted to engage in a debate with Sarbanes but Sarbanes refused to take on NCPAC. Terry Dolan wanted to debate Sarbanes. Well, hell, Terry Dolan wasn't even a candidate. And Sarbanes didn't fall for it but other candidates might. Long before the Republicans had nominated somebody all this had taken place.

NARRATOR: You were a member of the Miller Center Commission on the Presidential Nominating Process and you made the argument for the commission on the increase of individual contributions from one to five thousand or more, but you gave the reason there a little more fully. Do you want to say why you think that's important because of the amount of time the candidate spends for small gifts?

MR. ALEXANDER: Well, one reason is that the thousand dollar limit is rather low, particularly in presidential campaigns, maybe less so in House or Senate campaigns. But in any case in presidential campaigns where we're talking about multimillion dollar campaigns a thousand dollar contribution limit from an individual is rather low. I believe that with the good disclosure which we now have through the Federal Election Campaign Act that the problem of a larger contribution from individuals is not that great as long as the contribution is made in due course and recorded I think the public will have good information prior to the election and prior to the caucus or whatever as to where the money is coming from.

I believe that money from individuals is preferable to money from organizations and if you allow $5,000 for a PAC to give, I think you can allow $5,000 for an individual to give. That would infuse some more dollars into the system. I'm not as worried about the idiosyncrasies of Clement Stone or Stewart Mott or Norman Lear as I am about the institutional PAC giving, because when a corporation establishes a PAC or a labor union establishes a PAC it's more than $5,000. It may be fifty thousand jobs of that corporation. It may be facilities in thirty states. It means a heck of a lot more than just $5,000. In other words the leverage is more than just the dollars involved. But I'm not terribly concerned about some fat cats getting in the way Clement Stone did in 1972 when he gave $2 million to the Nixon campaign or Stewart Mott when he gave $400,000 to the McGovern campaign. Five thousand dollars is a lot of money but it's not gross in terms of some of the contributions that have come from individuals in the past.

NARRATOR: The argument that I thought the commission found very convincing was your argument where the challenger candidate spent all his time trying to get a whole collection of one thousand dollar contributions and it put the newly emerging political figure at a great disadvantage.

MR. ALEXANDER: Well, that's right. Incumbents have an advantage in any case, but particularly challengers have a hard time raising money and they need seed money. In presidential campaigns there is need for early money to establish an organization and to establish a fundraising mechanism to carry through the year before the election year or the year of nomination. And so that seed money is terribly important. Just think of what Baker and Bush would have to go through tomorrow if Reagan decided not to run.

QUESTION: It's very interesting and particularly helpful for me in thinking about NCPAC and accepting their right to be involved. In this matter of the amount that is spent, so many people gee whiz that to death—you're not among them and you contributed a lot to our understanding of why the amounts are what they are—has anybody ever developed some kind of index which would in some way standardize these campaign costs? Obviously there is inflation but that really doesn't account at all for the growth in technology. Has there ever been an effort to consider, say, the general increase in TV advertising, the amount of it, or the growth of political consultants and the cost of their being in business so that we can develop some kind of standard figure?

MR. ALEXANDER: Well, I'm glad you asked that because Citizen's Research Foundation, which is my organization, is now developing a proposal to establish an index of campaign costs. I don't know how successful it will be. It's a very difficult thing to do and you need time because you need at least two years to measure, or in presidential campaigns four years to measure, one against the other. The high cost of politics is a very real concern but I think it needs understanding. I mentioned the professionalization of politics. Years ago the party leader sort of put his ear to the ground and hoped to come up with a strategy that would help the candidate win. Today the first thing a candidate does is, as Jerry Ford said in 1976, "Before I even had a campaign manager, I had to have a lawyer and an accountant—a lawyer to give advice on complying with the law and an accountant to set up a system to comply with the law." When you think of professionalization you think of advertising people but you also have to think of computer people, not just in terms of direct mail but in terms of strategy of reaching various groups.

So we're into the application of high technology and that has caused the cost of campaigning to rise at a very rapid rate. And there's a price to be paid. Volunteerism is not as significant as it was. Years ago volunteers would go down to the party headquarters or the candidate's headquarters and they'd be willing to work, literally lick envelopes. Today that's all done by machine. You may have an idyllic situation here but I tell you that in the metropolitan areas with crime rates and the rest, it's very hard to compete with leisure time activities to get volunteers. And if you do get volunteers who are willing to canvass door to door, you may not get women to come out at night, particularly. Things like that are really deterrents to the kind of volunteer spirit that was the backbone of the American electoral system. Money has always been a scarce resource but now money is needed to buy the services of the skilled practitioners who bring a degree of professionalism. In addition to a lawyer and accountant you now need a pollster and a computer expert.

Professionalization is a very important thing to recognize in the rising cost of campaigns. Beyond that, of course, I think we're into a more highly competitive situation. The two party system is very competitive at least in presidential campaigns. if you look at all the money that's spent, as I did in my book, *Financing the 1980 Election*, I came up with the figure $1.2 billion in 1980 spent at the national, state, and local levels on all politics, including maintenance of the party system, but also all elective politics and ballot issues. The amount—$1.2 billion—is a fraction of one percent of our Gross National Product, of disposable personal income, of what governments spend at the federal, state, and local levels. Now that's hardly an answer for a candidate who needs money and wants to compete. But the fact is that we do not devote very much of our resources to politics. We spend more on chewing gum than we do on politics.

And so the costs of campaigns are bound to continue to rise. It is a very serious problem and the regulatory measures are very difficult to deal with because of Supreme Court decisions. What we have in the federal law is a jerry-built system based partly on congressional prerogatives, incumbent protection as they perceived it, modified by whatever the courts have said, plus amendments. The Federal Election Campaign Act was enacted in 1971 and there were seven amendments in 1974, 1976, and again in 1979. And Federal Election Commission decisions. And so we have a mixed system and it's not a rational system that any single person would devise.

QUESTION: Rather than compare the appropriate expenditure for campaigns to what we spend on chewing gum, I think instead of baseball and football and I think of the contest aspect of the passions engaged in partisan politics—so much more like the favorite hometown baseball team.

MR. ALEXANDER: But you know in talking about spending in politics you really have to look at the problem of apathy, the problem of stirring people up, the fact that expenditures are necessary in order to get people interested, the fact that expenditures are necessary even to keep the candidates' morale up. There was a campaign manager out in California who ran Pat Brown's campaign a number of years ago who once told me, we put up billboards across the state, that's the first step that we take because we have to prove that the candidate is a serious candidate—you have to make expenditures in order to bring in volunteers to do work and to be interested in the campaign. He said, a billboard never captured a vote but what it does is raise levels of confidence of the campaign, it says that it is a serious campaign, that you are able to raise money to spend money this way, and beyond that, he said, we used to put billboards in various strategic places where we knew damn well the candidate would be riding through and would see his picture and it would raise his morale and that of the campaign workers, just to see his picture up there.

QUESTION: Do you think the intent of these laws has been fulfilled by the disclosure element or do these PAC groups tend to evade that intent that financing public affairs should be public?

MR. ALEXANDER: Well, I think that first of all the disclosure laws have been quite successful. There are problems for scholars with some of the disclosure laws because we can't get all the information that we necessarily want, particularly on expenditures and how much is spent on advertising, on television, and so on from the campaign fund reports that are filed with the Federal Election Commission. But generally disclosure has been satisfactory and if the Federal Election Commission has been successful in any degree, it's in its administration of disclosure. I personally have felt that disclosure is the keystone of regulation and there is a right of the public to know before elections, not just the background and qualifications of the candidate, his program and promises, but also his sources of support. So I think that disclosure is essential and disclosure is pretty good right now. It might need a little fine tuning but it's essentially good.

Beyond that, however, you get into other questions. Political action committees are not very relevant in presidential campaigns, although in 1984 they may be more so than in 1980 or in 1976 because the AFL-CIO is making an endorsement, the National Education Association is making an endorsement, and you'll find new patterns of activity in the pre-nomination period that did not exist in 1980 or 1976 as a result of the efforts of those organizations to influence the outcome of the nomination. But except insofar as they engage in independent expenditures in presidential campaigns, PACs are most relevant in senatorial and congressional campaigns. And I think

PACs have to be recognized as solicitation systems, groups of like-minded people who are brought together, people who work for a corporation, people who belong to a union, and people who join an environmental group. PACs are part of this effort to broaden a base to seek out new contributors. I wish that candidates could reach contributors directly or parties could reach contributors more directly and PACs weren't these intermediaries in raising money, aggregating it, and then making contributions to candidates. But with the contribution limits, with the structure of politics as it is, PACs have turned out to be efficient and effective ways of raising money. With high costs, candidates want the PAC money. And the real problem with PACs is that they introduce this institutional bias that does get around the direct relationship between a candidate and his party or a citizen and his candidate.

QUESTION: What effect, if any, have you seen on the type of appointments the President has made, the type of policies that he has supported, that might be related to the way money is raised?

MR. ALEXANDER: In the case of candidates for President I think that there is probably less influence because a candidate for President has to appeal so broadly and cannot quite be so particularized as candidates for Senate or House may be and therefore are less subject to influence from their sources of support. I think that, generally speaking, people tend to give to candidates who are congenial and this of course applies to groups which also give to candidates who are congenial. In many cases they know that if the candidate is elected, they don't have to tell how to vote, they know how he'll vote on specific issues, at least on the big broad issues. I think where PACs are the most influential, where money is most influential, first, is in the pre-nomination period where candidates are chosen, where the party is not a vehicle. Alexander Heard wrote in *The Costs of Democracy* that the impact of money is greatest in the shadowland of the nomination phase where candidates are being nominated. A candidate is on his own. You know candidates are self-starters, they're entrepeteneurs, they're on their own to get the nomination. In many states, if you're talking about state laws, the parties can't participate, can't make pre-primary endorsements. So the candidate is really on his own to set up his own organization, do his own fundraising, his own media campaign, to get the nomination. Then once nominated the candidate feels he has to appeal beyond the party because there are a lot of independent voters out there, people who are typified as independent voters. The result is that the candidate then tries to appeal beyond just the party. And so in those circumstances the candidate is very much a lonely actor out there making his or her appeals.

QUESTION: Of the $1.2 billion can you estimate how much goes to the Republicans and how much to the Democrats, and if there is a big disparity would this affect your view of the desireability for a ceiling?

MR. ALEXANDER: At the federal level we do know the differences between Republican and Democratic spending. Of the $1.2 billion I can't give you a figure which says so much Republican, so much Democratic because that $1.2 billion includes ballot issues and party maintenance as well as campaigns for public office. Talking about campaigns for public officer in this country, over a four-year cycle we elect almost 500,000 public officials. In addition we have campaigns for nomination. Now a lot of these are not hotly contested. You may have trouble here in Charlottesville co-opting people to run for the school board or whatever and there may not be a campaign for nomination. But when you're talking about serious candidates for major office you're talking about money. So over a four-year period we tend to spend considerable amounts of money in that way.

To get to your specific question, I show in my book that it cost $275 million to elect a President, $275 million out of the $1.2 billion to elect a President. That included the pre-nomination costs, the costs of running the conventions, and the costs of running the general election campaigns. It cost about $240 million in 1980 to elect a Congress and so we're talking about $530 million, roughly, of that $1.2 billion at the federal level. And of those amounts the Democrats tend to spend more than Republicans but by diminishing percentages. In 1980 and even in 1982, in the congressional campaigns, Democrats outspent Republicans by about fifty-two to forty-eight percent. But there has been an important reason for that and that is Democrats have more registrations, Democrats hold more offices across the country, and getting a Democratic nomination has been worth more than getting a Republican nomination. So there is much more contesting for Democratic nominations throughout the country. So Democrats tend to spend more in primaries, Republicans spend more in general elections, but if you put it all together Democrats still spend more than Republicans. In that November election Republicans normally have the advantage that they're able to raise more money and spend more money and of course the Republican party nationally as well as in many states has decided advantages over the Democratic party nationally and in many states. You know what the case is here in Virginia. At the national level the Democratic National Committee, the Democratic Senatorial Campaign Committee, the Democratic Congressional Campaign Committee are outspent by the equivalent Republican committees by about eight to one.

NARRATOR: I think by your attention and interest you have paid Herb Alexander the highest possible tribute. I think he's shown that he continues to be the major figure in this area and we're terribly grateful to him for extending his trip east to come down here.

IN DEFENSE OF THE NOMINATING PROCESS

Richard M. Scammon

NARRATOR: We are pleased to welcome you to a Forum in the presidential nominating process series we're about to hold with Richard Scammon. In his case I have felt that I needed a little nemonic aid of some kind so I start by telling you that he's a graduate of the University of Minnesota, has a graduate degree from the University of Michigan; then his activities come in such rapid succession so that I do need help. He was research secretary in the radio office of the University of Chicago; he served with the office of military government in Germany from 1945 to 1948; he was chief of the Division of Research for Western Europe in the Department of State from 1948 to 1955; he was director of the Elections Research Center from 1951 to 1961 and then from 1965 to the present; he's been an election consultant of NBC News from 1964 to the present; he's been a consultant to the Department of State; he's been director of the Bureau of the Census of the Department of Commerce from 1961 to 1965; he was chairman of the United States delegation to observe elections in the USSR; chairman of the President's Commission on Registration and Voting Participation in 1963; member of the OAS electoral mission to the Dominican Republic 1966; chairman of the U.S. Select Committee of the Western Hemisphere Immigration from 1966 to 1968. I seem to associate him with the El Salvador election observation and the Kissinger Commission.

He's the co-author of a number of important works including fourteen volumes of the work *America Votes*; also *America at the Polls*. So we feel very privileged that one of the members of the Miller Center's Presidential Nominating Commission who, as has been true throughout his career, saw fit to assert some independent judgments alongside the views of the commission as a whole, would have an opportunity to develop his thoughts on that and any other related subjects in our discussion this afternoon.

MR. SCAMMON: It's been many years since I've been at the University of Virginia to speak. I must confess, Ken, that when I was here last I was introduced to a strange custom at this university. I went down to the basement of the hall we were meeting in and there were three doors there, men, women, and faculty. And I've never quite understood that. Perhaps I'll get elucidation here.

In talking briefly, as I will this afternoon before we invite your discussion on this presidential nominating system, I think we must remember our system has certain unique characteristics in the United States. It is bi-party oriented. We've had third party candidates for the presidency since the election of Abraham Lincoln in 1860. But we've never had a third party of any real moment since 1890, 1892, 1894 when the Populists collapsed in enthusiasm for free silver and joined the Democrats. We've had Bull Moosers and we've had LaFollette and we've had, even as recently as Anderson, independent candidates. But these were as individuals. They were not party oriented. Their support died immediately after the arrangements were finished, although in John's case he might go again next year. We'll wait and see on this. But basically it's a party operation. There's never been nonpartisanship of the kind that you get quite frequently in American municipal politics. It's been party oriented from the very beginning. Moreover it is the only one, I won't say the only one, there are a few odd places in American political life where the convention system still survives, in Virginia for example, in certain challenge primary solution states like Connecticut and Utah. But basically, beginning seventy or eighty years ago, we moved over from convention nominations to primary nominations. And these have dominated American politics in the past fifty years.

Even in the presidential process the introduction of the popular election of delegates has developed some of the same process for the selection of the presidential candidates that we use for state party nominations, but it still remains a concept of party in convention assembled, as the phrasing of the call goes. In this sense also, one must remember that it is an office for which you never vote. I once, in making speeches, used to offer a prize of one cigar if anyone could tell me who they had really voted for in the last presidential election and never could they do so because they couldn't remember the ten presidential electors of Minnesota or however it is in Virginia and the rest. Except once out west. This was at a student meeting and one student from a small state remembered that his father had been an elector and he could remember the names of the other two so he won the cigar. Since then I've not made the offer.

The indirect system of election is of course mainly a fiction of our constitutional system and remains so. In 1980 if you asked people who they voted for the day after election, and if they were willing to tell you, they would say Reagan or Carter or perhaps Anderson. Almost no one would reply to you with a long list of the names of the people for whom they actually cast a ballot. In fact now it's impossible to do so on most ballots in this country. You don't have the names of the electors even printed any more, you simply vote for the candidate you wish.

When we get into the selection process, then, we are talking about a process which has electoral aspects but is still formally a decision made by a group of delegates assembled for this purpose somewhere in America with due attention to television and all the rest. We make it, interestingly enough, in a highly traditional setting. I don't imagine there's very much left in American politics that is as traditional as the organization and conducting of the business of a national convention. The Committee on Nominations, the Committee on Resolutions, all properly put forward, the system of nominating the candidates, and calling the role in the states and so on. A man from the conventions of 1884 could come back next year and find very little had changed. Amplification of the human voice would probably be the biggest since the tremendous problem of the conventions of the nineteenth century was making yourself heard. Even though the halls were much smaller and the conventions delegates themselves might be well under one thousand, there were a lot of visitors. It's also interesting to note that the hall in those days was often Jerry built to house a convention. It wasn't much of a hall but it housed thousands of people, it managed all right. Now of course it would cost tens of millions of dollars and you would have to have hotels to house all the delegates and TV personalities. But in any event, the basic form remains fairly traditional.

What has changed substantially is the nature of the process of selecting a candidate. What originally began as a selection by a congressional caucus has now moved into a national campaign. The present one for example, which I think will probably be the longest that I will have ever seen, has been basically in

87

operation for six months already. And for any Democrat that probably really isn't soon enough because if the labor people are going to hold their own endorsing convention in the fall, as they've indicated they will, if the blacks are going to run their own candidate as they've indicated they may, if you have begun to extend the old caucus system of the conventions to an institutionalized year long factionalism in which you really set up factions like the Italian political parties do: left, moderate left, center, moderate right, far right then your campaign will begin as it does now for the House—on swearing-in day. It's because you've got to caucus all of these individual factions that are beginning to set up within the party, and particularly within the Democratic party since it tends to be more heterogeneous than the Republican.

So the great change in the last thirty years, basically in the years since Stevenson was nominated in 1952, is the shift from leadership nominations to popular nominations. The fact is that though Kefauver went out and won most primaries available to him, in 1952, the apparatus was strong enough to knife Kefauver and put in Stevenson, for better or for worse, I don't know.

That kind of situation has just disappeared. You don't find that any more. Now candidates announce very early. As a matter of fact even twenty years ago a candidate like Stassen who did announce way ahead was just laughed out of the hall. Maybe for other reasons too, but at least for the particular reason: "Oh, this is ridiculous." That the office seeks the man is probably one of the most ridiculous statements ever made about the presidency.

In this circumstance we now have all of the leading candidates out there, announced, ready to go. At least as far as the out-of-power party is concerned. For the in party of course the selection process is very different. Normally an elected incumbent after one term has no great trouble in getting renominated except for Lyndon Johnson. Even Hoover managed it in 1932 under very adverse conditions. As a matter of fact I suppose Ford would be the most immediate case of an elected incumbent who was very seriously challenged for renomination. But normally we're talking of the challenging party and not the incumbent party as one which is off and running two years ahead of time. Mondale and Kennedy, for example, had organized well before the 1982 elections their own private political action committees which were moving about making small contributions to various candidates to help their campaigns, obviously in the hope that bread cast upon waters would not come back as a soggy lump but as active delegates when the appropriate time came. But the candidates are out there working, they're crisscrossing Iowa and getting ready for the first primary in New Hampshire and the long list of primaries that will follow through June before the convention.

The selection process, moreover, becomes highly nationalized now. Because the old concept that Teddy White used to love to talk about, about "Indiana votes as Indiana" is plain passe'. The blacks in Indiana vote the way the blacks in Washington, D.C., do. The trade unionists in Indiana vote the way their union is going to vote in Michigan. The idea that Indiana has a special interest apart from that of the country is just not there. Occasionally you'll find someone like Cranston floating a balloon and getting the local support, but basically that's because if you don't get even the local support of your own state, people will think you aren't worth a damn anywhere else and they'll probably be right and they won't support you.

But the staffs are being built up here in Washington, the schedules are being arranged, the money's being arranged, the whole thing is really in pretty heavy water already as far as 1984 is concerned. How this is going to operate through the next fifteen months until the convention is a little hard to say. We are starting earlier than normal, particularly on the Democratic side with that labor endorsement. But it's going to be a little hard to maintain public interest although I must confess perhaps we really aren't talking about a public yet. We're talking about the afficionados who are being activated, not the general public. Most of *them* probably wouldn't care.

But the pollsters are already starting: Democrats, Republicans, who would you prefer for your candidate? Particularly on the Democratic side of course. And the pollsters will have also been operating on the Republican side if Mr. Reagan does not run—"Who would you like to see as your party's candidate?—as they have done in past years. With the general acceptance of polling, at least as some kind of measure of the public mind, this will be an important part of any campaign strategy. Mondale is ahead of Glenn, the pollsters say, but Glenn would run better in November than Mondale would, and then the Glenn people will reproduce and send around copies as their *raison d'etre* in the campaign.

The selection process as always will feature the fact that running for the nomination is not running for the election and running for the election is not running for the nomination. You've got two very different constituencies here. The people who decide who goes to the conventions, the activists, the militants in the parties are usually, in fact more than that, are almost *always* much more to the left than the party rank and file in the Democratic party and much more to the right than the party rank and file in the Republican party. A selection process really built upon the party activists is a selection system of extremes. The major thing which I would submit tends to make candidates veer to moderation in the center is the participation of more and more people in the presidential preferential primaries. The party left to itself would nominate Jesse Helms and McGovern. I'm making an overstatement but not by much. They've done it twice with Goldwater and Mc-Govern as it is. But it's the necessity of putting together a coalition which will win fifty million votes and therefore win the White House that leads, one might say, to the triumph of greed over ideology and moves people to the center.

Under these circumstances commitment to the activist groups is demanded of the candidates for at least the two years before the election. Sometimes longer. They're there. There's not much you can do about it, they're going to work hard, they're trying to improve their position in the polls, they're talking to the leading personalities in the party in every state in the union. But after the ball is over, after the nomination is won, centrism emerges.

The operation of nominating a candidate becomes much longer than it ever used to be in a society that's much better equipped to communicate than it ever was, so that we will get inundated with the presidential campaign for a long, long time. Now mind you, this long campaign must be put in perspective. It's not as long as the British campaign. The British campaign never stops because in any parliamentary system you're never sure that the leader of the government, the prime minister, may not call an election—snap—like that. The result is that the candidates in Britain for the next parliamentary election are probably at least seventy-five percent chosen, nominated already because they don't know when they have to go. We have the blessings, or the lack thereof, of a firm schedule and so we know exactly when we're going to nominate and when we're going to elect and so on.

But I'm always bemused by the claim that we have a very

long campaign and nobody else does. The campaign between the CDU and the SPD in Germany, like that in Britain, is ongoing and constant. There are even regular party broadcasts for four years, for each political party so they can announce what they think about things. We're actually really blessed by a relatively short campaign even if it's two years long.

But here the media treatment, the polling treatment, the *Meet the Press, Issues and Answers* kind of treatment, is combined with what you might call the public level—with the level of maneuverability which is, bring in all the Kentucky county chairmen and party leaders. I want to meet with them in Louisville in three weeks time. And they'll usually come because they want to see what the product is. And this is a constant drain upon everybody who's been in politics. Now if you've been in politics for a while it's not as great a drain as if you were starting afresh, say somebody like Wendell Willkie, who in 1940 moved with the speed of light, moved up from a three percent vote among Republicans in April to be nominated in June, and this before television.

The selection process varies a great deal, as you know, from state to state. But the majority of people will have an opportunity in the spring of 1984 to vote at least a preference. They may not be able to control the actual selection of delegates. This may come through a different process. But in my own mind I'm convinced that the mere expression of a preference in the primary for a candidate is just as important as who gets elected to be delegate. If one candidate comes through those preference primaries with a clear lead, it is only the most ideological or the most unseeing of party leaders who will support the candidate who got thirty percent over the candidate who got sixty-five percent. Most party leaders want to win. They'd like to win under the old label or they'd like to win for an ideology that they feel comfortable with, but most of all they want to win. Those on the ideological swing of the party system would like to win but that isn't that important. But for them to try to control a nomination and put onto the ballot the candidate with the thirty percent rather than the candidate with the sixty-five percent would be almost totally self-defeating in modern American politics.

So the votes in the primaries will have a major effect in deciding who wins the nominations. The major effect will come not only directly between who gets the headlines—"Reagan Triumphs In New Hampshire," whatever it may be—but they'll also come from the desire of success-seeking politicans to align themselves with somebody who can win. This is not an unknown phenomenon in politics in this country or anywhere else. You'll see it again. I would hope we do not get led astray in the spring of 1984 by constantly referring to the delegates who've been elected. These are not unimportant obviously, particularly if they're under strong discipline. But it is really less important than who emerges in the public opinion polls and in the presidential primaries themselves as a clear leading candidate. It's a democratic process, a rather brawly, sometimes nasty, sometimes dirty, time-consuming, exhausting process, but if you're going to poop out, poop out in Wisconsin in April 1984 and not in the White House after you get elected.

There is something elemental about an American presidential campaign. It is not for the weak or the weak stomached. It is not for the slow. It's not for those who can't think fast. It is an obstacle course. This is the great advantage in the American selection process. You don't approach the White House via the condescension of an elite. You approach the White House because you got down there in the bear pit and wrestled with the bear. Hopefully you won but at least you wrestled with the bear. Let me stop with that high level note to see what sort of questions and comments we might want to embark on.

QUESTION: Mr. Scammon, you gave a lot of credit to the party apparatus for the nomination of Adlai Stevenson in 1952. Don't you think that that brilliant, that utterly brilliant waffling that he gave to the delegates as Governor of Illinois welcoming them to Chicago had a great deal to do with it? It was the greatest speech I ever heard.

MR. SCAMMON: With all respect, I don't think so. You were listening to the speech. Many of the delegates were not and if they did hear it they weren't paying attention and if they were paying attention they didn't give a damn. The fact of the matter is that they were not there to evaluate speeches. And it was a beautiful speech. I remember it. It *was* beautiful. No, this would not have had that much effect. One of the major reasons was that many of the leadership didn't like Kefauver, they didn't want him, they thought he was a challenging element and they were dubious about him in many ways. Stevenson was a certified intellectual who had been elected along with Paul Douglas when the organization in Chicago felt that they needed a little polish to get some of the tarnish off the machine. But no, quite frankly, with all respect to your question, I just don't believe that would have affected more than a few votes among the delegates.

QUESTION: I have a question, Mr. Scammon, on the use of television projections as they effect going timewise to the Pacific Coast. Do they or do they not influence the electorate out in the new time zone as opposed to—

MR. SCAMMON: Well, you really shouldn't ask me that question because I'm a party at interest. As you know the story was that hundreds of thousands of voters on the West Coast didn't bother to vote because they figured Reagan had won, because the announcement had been made at eight-fifteen Eastern time, which is five-fifteen California time. The fascinating thing is that the true story never caught up. What was the true story? Voter turnout in the East zone where so many polls had closed actually dropped off more than it did on the West Coast. Now you can argue a lot of reasons why this happened, but I think that actually people pay little attention to any of these things. And even the fact that the voter turnout declined less on the West Coast than on the East Coast I don't think had much to do with projections.

But what has been suggested is that if this is a problem, it happens only in the landslide years. I've done six elections for NBC and this has happened to us three times, where we've had a landslide election, 1964, 1972 and 1980. This of course is basically a problem of the time zones. Or if this seems too dramatic to you, collapse the Eastern into the Central and the Pacific into the Mountain and have two time zones, and then everybody could agree to have a universal poll closing time at maybe eight o'clock in the west, nine o'clock in the east. The universal poll closing time is the easy solution but as of now that would mean that you would have to close the polls probably no later than six or seven o'clock in California and people might not like that. The Canadians have thought of this and they have put up legislation on it, but the trade unions out in British Columbia have opposed it on the grounds that the voting would have to stop about four-thirty in the afternoon, because as you know the Canadians have an extra hour and a half on their time zone scale over and above what we have.

The other possible arrangement is not to count any ballots until Wednesday morning. Now this would drive the politicians up a wall. It's used in England in about half the constituencies. They gather all the ballots, they close at ten o'clock and in the country areas they gather all the ballots in the county hall and wait. And then the next day at nine o'clock in the morning they start counting. That's a possibility.

No action has been taken by the Congress, which of course has full power to regulate this. And perhaps they really don't think it's that much of a problem. But again, I'm really not the one you should ask because I am a party at interest.

QUESTION: I know that the nomination of Wendell Willkie was far off the normal course, it opens up a lot of possibilities inasmuch as that's not typical, as you point out. How many people in the country do you think, say at this moment, are possible presidential candidates? That have got all that it takes in their backgrounds?

MR. SCAMMON: Well, for the party in the White House, it is obviously easier. Really if you went at it now for 1984, the primary decision obviously is Mr. Reagan's as to whether to run or not. If he decides to run certainly he'll be renominated, no question. If he decides not to run, and you have a Republican open shot, I suppose half a dozen would occur to mind. On the Democratic side you have a short list of fifty. Now that's not an effective short list. There are three leaders at the present time.

QUESTION: Now that seems a rather long list to me.

MR. SCAMMON: Well, but you never can tell where the lightning is going to strike. You really can't tell. People come up and go down with great rapidity in this modern day of communication. It would seem to me that if the Republicans had to nominate, you might be able to limit it to Dole, Baker, and Bush, maybe an outside chance for Kemp; no, not an outside chance for Kemp. Too far out. No, Kemp and McCloskey in California would be equivalent distances from the center of the party. On the Democratic side the top three, Cranston, Glenn, and Mondale at the present time, plus a fairly large number of possibles if you got deadlocked. Of course, you could also add to the Republican list if a deadlocked convention should result.

Now, one intriguing thing is that since the war, since the elections of 1948 we've had very rare instances of nominating conventions going more than one ballot. Actually, none since Stevenson was the Democratic nominee after three ballots in 1952. Consensus develops much faster. A hundred years ago when the party leaders met in many cases they hadn't seen each other for four years. We didn't have rapid communication, unless they were members of Congress: Hello, how are you, oh, I remember you, very interesting, how are things?

94

And it would take you a little while to maneuver and they'd go forty, fifty, ballots without any problem at all. That didn't mean that there were forty or fifty separate makings of a judgment. It meant that this was a way to kill time while the leadership tried to get together to work out something.

But that won't happen now. It's too exposed. It's too public. Things move much too fast. And if we now got even a second or a third ballot it would be unusual in terms of contemporary American political practice. I would think that most of the possibles are probably out in the open now, men like Gary Hart or Askew or Hollings. Udall has quit. Brown has been pushed out by the voters of California. Kennedy has been in and out. So I think really your effective list is probably three maybe four on the Republican side and really no more than six or eight on the Democratic, who are really capable of being nominated. But you have to provide the saving clause, like "anything *can* happen," but it usually doesn't.

QUESTION: I was really leading up to another question there because we're starting here with a country of two hundred and twenty-five million or something and we've got twelve possible people. Now, what are the chances of getting a good nominee out of that?

MR. SCAMMON: I wouldn't apply this word "good". Good is a judgment in this case. Good for what? Good for the Republic? Good for the election? Good for my ideology?

QUESTION: What is good for the Republic?

MR. SCAMMON: Oh, what is good for the Republic? You'll get some general agreement, and the more general, the more the agreement and the more specific, the less the agreement. Protectionism, for example, is this good or bad for the Republic? In this group you'd find it probably generally rejected. If they had a meeting of local 209 of the UAW it would be approved. Policy towards Israel, policy towards El Salvador, policy towards the Soviet Union, policy towards social security, policy towards bilingual education in the schools which is a wonderful issue because you can never identify whether it's liberal or conservative.

Or others: What is a "good" policy on abortion? School bussing? Gun control? Fifty years ago what was a "good" policy on prohibition? Ninety years ago what was a "good" policy on silver coinage? "Good" depends on what you think is good. Now if you mean good in the sense of winning that's much more specific. But that isn't what you had in mind.

QUESTION: No, I had the other in mind but I'll admit it's an impossible question.

QUESTION: Could you say just a little bit about the thirty-six primaries? In order to prove his mettle and emerge as the strong, tested figure that you described, do you have to run the gamut of thirty-six primaries?

MR. SCAMMON: Well, you can probably eliminate Rhode Island, Vermont, and a few others, but you have to run in all the big ones unless you can convincingly exclude yourself for some good reason. Moreover, you never can be quite sure. Somebody's going to run a write-in campaign for you and you end up with fourteen votes and you look bad, because there it is, big on the screen, you know: so and so, two hundred and twenty-five thousand; Scammon, fourteen. Oh God, they really creamed him, didn't they? You can't really run away from it. You really can't in a big state. Some of the smaller states, nobody would blame you if you don't run in South Dakota, but the big ones—New York, if they determine to do it that way in New York; California particularly; Illinois early; Texas, if the parties decide to do this; Florida; Pennsylvania; and Ohio. Every one of them has had some form of presidential preference primary. It may vary a little because laws may be changed in the next fifteen months or so. But if you ducked any substantial number of those you would either be afraid, number one, or sure you weren't going to win, number two.

QUESTION: Doesn't this give the great advantage to the unemployed politician, to be able to run in that many primaries?

MR. SCAMMON: Well, it never stopped Senator Kennedy. Right now four of the six announced Democrats are senators. John Kennedy was very straightforward on this. He never made the mistake of thinking the Senate was more important than the White House and he was going for the White House and that was it. By and large with modern communication you probably could get by with doing both, being in the Senate at the appropriate time and campaigning. You don't have to be unemployed. If you're unknown you have to—now, Carter parlayed this very nicely because he didn't do anything after he left the governorship of Georgia but run for President and he worked very hard at it. Mondale's doing the same. But no, I don't think that this would invalidate, given TV advertising and given the fact that you've got some time and given the fact that you can get somebody to loan you a jet, I don't really think that this would be a major obstacle. It might be easier if you were unemployed, but not essential.

QUESTION: Dick, I was wondering what your evaluation was of the Democratic party's latest attempt at rules reform, the Hunt Commission, the rules changes?

MR. SCAMMON: Well, I would think the addition of non-committed, elected officials provides a very intriguing leaven to the activists, because nothing makes a man more centrist than having to go out and win an election. Like Johnson's observation about the prospect of hanging: hanging, it concentrates the mind wonderfully. The viewpoint of any elected official from alderman up to President is different than the view of the ideological activist who is out there shouting for the cause. Because the elected official has had to put together a coalition. He's had to compromise and say, "Come let us reason together, let me make you an offer you can't refuse," something of this sort. The net result is that he has a different viewpoint. Many congressmen didn't want to go to the conventions of the past because they didn't want to get caught in the middle, say between the Carter people and the Kennedy people in their own district. They wanted a hundred percent of the Democrats voting for them in their primary. They didn't want to be cut out. They didn't want to have the losing side put a candidate up against them in the September nominating primary in their own district because they went their own way. So I would think this will be an interesting leaven. How much of a leaven, I don't know.

Now the other problem which deals with trying to force parties either to hold their primaries in a certain window of time or to keep other people from crossing over is a different story. I don't know how that's going to work out. In the recent primaries in Chicago, for example, for mayor, ninety-nine percent of the voters took a Democratic ballot. One percent took a Republican ballot, which means of course it's a total crossover. In Philadelphia in May when they are also having a mayoral primary, black and white, you can't do that. That's a fixed primary and you can't cross over and Goode ought to beat Russo on that basis simply because Republicans can't cross over and vote for Russo even if they wanted to.

QUESTION: I want to go back to an earlier question which you answered in terms of values. I want to push you in terms of qualities. You drew a distinction between getting nominated and getting elected, which I think is valid. And just to project that further, what qualities do you need in a President, what qualities do you need to get nominated, what qualities do you need to get elected?

MR. SCAMMON: They're the same. Basically if you were to summarize them quickly you'd say brains and guts. Without both you've got very little shot. If you're stupid, you aren't going to make it. They can't prop you up enough if you're stupid. No matter how good your speech writer is, no matter how good your advisers ("Don't say that, Mr. President"), no matter how many people whisper in your ear, in the modern communicative world you just can't make it unless you're good on your feet and you've got some brains. The guts go without saying. You're never going to win anything like the presidency if you're really frightened of it.

QUESTION: Reagan isn't that bright, though.

MR. SCAMMON: Yes, I think he is.

QUESTION: Really? But he's made enough gaffes in all the talks and so forth.

MR. SCAMMON: This kind of thing, though, is what I would call the folkish gaffe. It's the kind of gaffe you make and people sort of smile. But if you really made a mistake—a bad one, then it would hurt. But most of the things that Reagan says, his malapropism, whatever it may be, the journalists will remember them because they're good stories, but no, the general public wouldn't. Some of his stuff is just marvelous, though. Going out to buy four valentines for his wife on Valentine's Day. Very nice, very nice. And his ability to conduct these give and take sessions is first rate though nobody has been as good as John Kennedy. The wit of Kennedy and the sharpness I don't think has been replicated since. But Reagan is pretty good at this for the masses, for the masses now, we're not talking about the sort of academic intellectual journalistic fraternity. This is a different group. Basically, the academic journalistic intellectual fraternity is maybe five percent, but the people who bowl regularly are the ones that count.

QUESTION: Seems like they're rather naive. If President Reagan decides not to be the candidate again, and I'm not too excited about Baker, Bush, or Dole, what would be the possibility or is it impossible for a person like George Shultz to get the nomination?

MR. SCAMMON: It would be very difficult for Shultz to get it. Shultz would be generally regarded I think, within the party at least, as staff. He's a person who fills a kind of job as secretary of state and fills it very well. But in terms of color, less colorful than Kissinger. You couldn't very well nominate Kissinger, even if he were born in the United States, which he wasn't, but no, I think they would go first to Bush for two reasons. First, because he's there. There *is* a "there" there. It's named Bush. And secondly, because in the last thirty years since the death of Mr. Roosevelt after the war, there has been a growing tradition of the vice president as having a sort of first refusal on the nomination. That doesn't mean he always gets it. But if you went back fifty years in American politics, the idea of a vice president becoming a presidential candidate next time was not really thought of seriously. But now as we have much more nationalized our political scope, this has become very real and Bush would have a good deal of support. He's a Yalie from Texas and that's a very nice combination politically. But I wouldn't say that it oils his way, and that's a horrible pun, I know. But Bush would probably have a considerable lead, particularly if the President did not announce his decision until relatively late. I remember when Coolidge made his announcement, it was in August of 1927, when he announced he "did not choose to run," which is a beautiful phrase in itself, but this was in August. I would think the President would probably have to do something by that time, if he were not going to run. Now if he doesn't say anything people will assume he will run, obviously. If he does not make an announcement by Labor Day, you're only six months ahead of the primaries. Even the filing requirements are such that you really have to become active by the fall, unless you want to do a Lyndon Johnson, as he tried it with incredible reticence. A man like Johnson was never known as a shy or reticent personality. The way in which he sort of just didn't want to ever say he was a candidate, it was as though he was running back in 1904 or something of the sort. I presume Reagan will say something by the early fall simply, as I say, if he's not going to run, to let his colleagues get started. He has an obligation to them, let them get organized and get underway. If he says nothing by that time it would seem pretty clear to me he will run.

QUESTION: I was going to ask if you'd care to go bowling after we break up here?

MR. SCAMMON: I'm afraid I'm not a bowler.

QUESTION: I wonder if you'd comment on the frequently tossed up question of constitutional change for the six year term, the one term presidency, four years for the House of Representatives and so forth.

MR. SCAMMON: Well, I may be too much of a traditionalist and have watched the system for too long and it seems that it does work pretty well. I put you back to 1931. If the American people in 1931 really believed that Hoover would be in office for three more years, I think you would have shaken the social fabric of America very seriously, very seriously. And those of you who remember the Depression, I remember it as a kid in Chicago and Minneapolis, the feelings of the people were very strong. They didn't know who they wanted in his place and some of them wouldn't even blame Hoover personally. But if you had had three more years of Hoover in the White House you really would have had difficulties. To some people this would apply today with Reagan. I would say that the ability to throw out somebody you don't want and replace him with somebody in whom you have more confidence, whether correctly placed or not being irrelevant, is a very valid part of the democratic process. I don't think you'd have to go as far as the old original British chartists, that is to say, annual parliaments, you elect them every year. But the idea of a congressman being elected every two years I like, I think that's fine. They say, well, he can't do anything, that's fine too. The fact is that many members of Congress do stay a good deal longer than just that two years. But it does give you an opportunity to throw the rascal out if you think he's a rascal. And of course with Reagan or with Hoover or with any other President, people will make this argument and say, well, he can't accomplish his program, but that raises a nice question. Why should he accomplish his program? This premises that his program is per se good, as your question about the character of the President. I don't premise it's either good or bad. What I premise is that it be subject to review by his peer group, which is every other citizen. In fact he can vote on it, too. I've not been moved by those who feel that by some gimmick, lengthening this term, shortening this term, this sort of thing, that you're going to change the nature of the political process. I really don't believe that. I respect their judgment and many of them are very accomplished people and they feel very strongly about this. I think it's a searching after something which, to my mind, is more gimmickry than it is reality.

QUESTION: I'd like to say, I would like to suggest that your definition of what it takes to be a candidate, being guts and intelligence, you have denied by your answer to me. And so I would like to say what quality is it that Reagan and the other ones have which intellectuals don't consider intelligence?

MR. SCAMMON: All of us tend to think people who follow our line of reasoning are pretty intelligent. Brains and guts I give you as a quick answer for qualifications. But obviously, whether you think that the individual candidate has got the brains depends on your judgment as to what the brains consist of. So this becomes personal as well as obviously identifiable.

QUESTION: But it's not abstract logic. What is it?

MR. SCAMMON: Instinct. It's probably a combination of instinct, prejudice, patriotism in an obscure way, all sorts of odds and ends which add up to why the average voter votes, with logic, being abstract or not, being an attribute only of Mr. Spock in television stories. Logic is not necessarily why you vote the way you do, even if you could establish what the logical choices were, which is a nice question in itself.

QUESTION: Some years ago, Mr. Scammon, I think you were widely quoted as saying at that time that elections were still won by the unyoung, the unblack, and the unpoor. Is that a direct quote and is it still true and will it be true in 1984?

MR. SCAMMON: Yes, it is true. The poor—there aren't enough truly poor to elect anybody. The fact of the matter is that poverty is not an issue which is voted on by the poor. Poverty is an issue which is the moral problem of the middle class. It is the middle class who vote on questions of poverty and if you vote one way or the other that's what gives you the answer. You could add up all the 1980 voters under the poverty level in America, you could add up all the 1980 black voters in America, many of whom would duplicate the poor of course, and you could add all under thirty voters in 1980 and you'd go down to glorious defeat. It's a middle class middle aged society.

QUESTION: If the blacks, as their leaders are now talking about, agree on what they call a national favorite son and make some strong effort in the primaries next year, what effect will that have on the Democratic nomination?

MR. SCAMMON: I can't think of any. The blacks were all united behind Carter, a white man, and he lost. As a matter of fact, you know, black unity is a relatively recent thing. In 1960 when Kennedy ran, Nixon carried the black wards in a city like Atlanta, because the Democratic candidates in the state of

Georgia at that time had at the top of their ticket their slogan, "White Supremacy for the Right." Now it says, "Democrats for the Right." That's progress. Basically, in an election system numbers count. One and one is two. It's not two hundred and twenty-eight point nine. And under these circumstances the national black vote amounts to about nine or ten percent. It is concentrated in certain large states which makes it useful in the electoral college and it might be expanded a little, as it was in Chicago on a particular local situation where voting for a black candidate was made a major issue. I may add parenthetically the voting in Chicago that we watched was one of the most polarized recent elections I've seen in this country except in the Deep South, only comparable to the delta district of Mississippi in the elections of 1982.

But if the blacks were to unite behind a white candidate, then of course you get a problem as to who elected him. I remember the old questions in 1960. Who elected Jack Kennedy? Catholics said, "We elected Jack Kennedy." The blacks said "We elected Kennedy." The trade unions said, "We elected Kennedy. Middle class white Anglo-Saxon Protestants like me elected Kennedy. And anybody who voted for Kennedy could say they elected him because he won by a margin of only a hundred thousand votes and under those conditions everybody's a king maker. What you can say is that it would be very difficult for the Democrats to win the presidency *without* the black vote or *without* the Catholic vote or *without* the Jewish vote or *without* the trade union vote. As a matter of fact if you ruled all those out you wouldn't have a winner.

But for the blacks to put up a candidate of their own or for the women to put up a candidate of their own, as the labor unions have started to do, gets back to this problem which I spoke of, of institutional factionalization. There's always factionalization in a heterogeneous party like the Democratic party, but the more institutionalized the factionalization, the more difficult you make it for the leadership to meld interests together. Because individual interests become more than just the interest of the individual. They become the interests of the group and they come up to the state of flag-flying and marching in the streets and you get real problems. Blacks may do this, they may not. It depends a lot on the candidate. If they put up Mayor Bradley of Los Angeles, like the Republicans did with Senator Brooke some years ago these are politicians who happen to be black instead of Polish, or Jewish, or Italian, or

Wasp or whatever and there's a big difference between them and a black politician seen as only concerned about blacks.

QUESTION: You kept circling one thing, you said brains, guts, I add a third, money and do you think the political action committee, say, "improvement" in our election process is pushing things into a more fractured state and if so, how do you get rid of the political action committees now that they are institutionalized?

MR. SCAMMON: Oh, I doubt if you do. They are institutionalized only in the sense that it's a new way of doing it. One of my colleagues did a survey of the election of 1928 and pointed out that one third of the money on both sides of the 1928 election for President came in contributions of more than five thousand dollars and that was when five thousand dollars is a lot more than it is now. The money's always going to be there. Actually, I'm not anti-labor and I see no reason to be anti-PAC. Because remember that half of the biggest PACs are labor PACs. It is also true that more PAC money goes to Democrats than to Republicans.

But the PACs are there. I rather like the PACs because the parties really don't mean much. You can be anything. Take Virginia. You even have had a governor who first was elected on one ticket and then on another, you know. What reality is there to party lines here? The fact is that here politics are much more a matter, as they are so often in the states, of history, personality and issues, not party label issues. Those are secondary. I don't think I'd give money to a party any more. I'd give it to a candidate or I'd give it to a political action group.

Tell you a story. In 1940 when Willkie was running against Roosevelt I was doing a radio show in New Jersey and on Sunday night we were in New York and I was wandering up Fifth Avenue past the public library. On Fifth Avenue and Forty Second where the public library is there are two great stone lions out front. That night about seven or eight o'clock on a Sunday night, one was the Democratic lion and one was the Republican lion. And the Willkie people all gathered in front of their lion and they'd get up and make speeches, and the Democrats would gather in front of their Roosevelt lion, they'd get up and make speeches and they'd speak for about thirty seconds and somebody would tug on you "Dammit, it's my turn, get down." Actually it was a rather moving experience. No organization, no police, no chairman, no banner, just people. But that was a long time ago and now if I want influence in politics I don't go back to the lion. Wouldn't dare because you'd probably get mugged before the speech was done. So I'd send a check.

There are so many political action committees going now, ideologicals, single interest, class organizations, and so on. I ought to be able to find one that represents my interests. And the system works, I think, fairly well. Because you get the broad party coalescing which is essential at arriving at a choice and then you get the individual interests expressing themselves as they always will, now often through PACs.

One more great advantage of the PACs is the money's up front. You can see where the money is. You never used to be able to do that in American politics, but every PAC has to report. And they do report because else they're going to be caught in real trouble with the law. In fact I know businessmen who say the PACs protect them because they used to get sandbagged by candidates who will say, "Now, we put you down for ten thousand," and now they give to a PAC and the PAC will publish the list of everything. I don't know whether you've ever seen any of the lists for PACs but most of them give very small sums. I watched one for one industrial group that supported forty candidates and I think they gave each one a thousand dollars.

QUESTION: Eugene McCarthy when he was here said at least when Clement Stone supported Nixon you knew who Stone was and you knew what he stood for. With the PACs you have no idea, other than the name on the masthead, who the individuals are.

MR. SCAMMON: Of course you know who they're for. If the American Home Builders Association contributes a lot of money to a candidate, you know what they're interested in. They're interested in a higher rate of return on the investment in home building, they're interested in cheap lumber, they're interested in every single bill that's going to get in there and help them. Same thing is true with the unions. I don't mind self-interest. I like the idea that greed is identified and then you can say well, all right, we can understand that. Whatever the interest is, I don't object to interests active in politics, I object to interests under the table. The old system of politics was there's a white envelope with a lot of hundred dollar bills in it and when I get up bend over and pick it up off the floor, this sort of thing. The great advantage of the PACs is the money's out front, you can see it. And if Gene can't identify the interest represented. I don't see how anybody else can miss it.

QUESTION: I just want to say from experience in Washington with the PACs that I wanted to corroborate what you said. All the PACs I was familiar with, the corporate PACs, gave very little money, gave it to very many people to hedge their bets to agree that this made the whole thing almost cancel itself out by the time you put them all together.

MR. SCAMMON: But what they also do is they protect the candidate because if your PAC could give a candidate fifty thousand dollars and did, then the premise that this guy's vote was really being bought by the PAC would have a good deal more validity. But if he collects a thousand dollars each from fifty PACs, some of which are antithetical to one another, either they're making a mistake or he's doing it the better way. A large contribution from a PAC, if I were a candidate, I'd be very dubious about it unless my interest in that matter was already identified. Moreover most of these PACs do not support new starters. They support incumbents because they've got a track record for the incumbent. You don't know what some bright young lawyer is going to do when he gets there. An incumbent has a voting record.

Usually in politics, I don't know how it is here, but normally in politics you find somebody who agrees with you and give him the money. And the more qualified he is the more likely he is to win an election. This is an investment process in a PAC. You say well, we've got a bright young fellow here in the forty-third Ohio, which doesn't exist, the man who represents it now is seventy-six years old, he falls asleep, he's got troubles and he's due to go and we've got a bright young lawyer here who's thrity-five years old and willing to spend a year of his own time campaigning, which is important, his family is well known in the area and so on, hasn't got any enemies, married, got four kids and so on. Let's talk to him. They'll talk to him and maybe they'll invest in him. But more often they'll go with a known quantity.

QUESTION: Let me ask a question to draw out one dimension that you haven't talked much about today. If you were to be a born again populist and reformer and depart from what has been the gravamen of a lot of your discussion today, namely trying to interpret and in a way defend things as they are, what changes would you favor in the presidential nominating process?

MR. SCAMMON: My personal preference would be a popular vote with or without this convention system. I'd just follow the French system, a ballot and a run-off if nobody got fifty percent—or maybe even forty.

QUESTION: Would you have anything before or after it? Would you have any pre-primary?

MR. SCAMMON: Entirely up to the party. Let them do whatever they want. As long as the power of nomination, in the final analysis, was in my hands in picking the top two for the runoff, I'd follow more or less the French system.

QUESTION: So the conventions would go?

MR. SCAMMON: They might or they might stay, either way or perhaps they would become endorsing mechanisms.

QUESTION: What do you say to the people who say that we have a national tendency and trait of trying something on a small scale and when it doesn't work then we blow it up to a big scale and that is what we would do with a national primary? All primaries don't work, in other words, according to this argument.

MR. SCAMMON: Basically that it isn't of major importance because we aren't going to change the system anyway. Any personal preferences I may have for popular election—or nomination, are really irrelevant. Basically, we are going to keep the system we've got. Modify it a bit, perhaps, but that is about all.

QUESTION: Are you saying do away with the electoral system as well? Do away with the electoral college, do away with the states in voting for the presidency?

MR. SCAMMON: Again, my personal preference would be simplistic—a national election by our whole people. But candor compels me to say I don't think that is likely. I don't feel strongly about this in the sense that I think it is the only thing that counts. As a matter of fact if you wanted to have direct elections you could even do it now, indirectly, because every state in the union has the right to decide how its own electors are going to be chosen. And if the state of Virginia wanted to proportionalize its electors in the next meeting of the electoral college, they could do so. If they wish to. Of course they won't because then nobody would campaign in the state and no money would come in. In Minnesota, where you've got ten electors, it would always be five to five, six to four or four to six. It would never get up to seven to three or three to seven. The result is that everybody would bypass you with the campaign money because when you've got ten or nothing that's big casino and you've got to make it. But if you really wanted popular direct election you could get it that way and it would be almost the same thing, not entirely. You'd still have problems.

NARRATOR: We certainly appreciate your visit and look forward to the next one.

MR. SCAMMON: Thank you. It was a great pleasure for me.

CONCLUSION

As we bring the third volume of the Gund Lectures to a close, a host of issues remain open. While not surprising, the persistence of different views suggests that the subject of the nominating process, as with many political questions, is infinitely more complex than we initially supposed.

The three volumes have provided a broad overview of the theory and practice of the selection process, the continuing debate over broadening or narrowing questions of reform and a careful review of leading constitutional, political, and economic issues. We have turned to the best qualified American observers and discovered significant differences in their viewpoints. In providing the breadth of coverage the three volumes offer, we have intended to supplement the recommendations of the Miller Center commission, not contradict them. It would be our hope that the scholar, political leader, and concerned citizen might draw on these several sources of ideas and proposals in forming personal conclusions.

At some future date, we may in a fourth volume carry our work to the point of more definitive conclusions formulated in Rotunda Lectures and papers by leading authorities. Until that time, the Commission Report and three Gund Lectures volumes may serve as working texts for those who grapple with these complicated issues. It is only fair to add that none of our work would have been possible without the generous assistance of the George Gund Foundation and its Executive Director, James Lipscomb.

COMMISSION ON THE PRESIDENTIAL NOMINATING PROCESS

EXECUTIVE BOARD*

Melvin R. Laird
Commission Co-chairman

Adlai E. Stevenson, III
Commission Co-chairman

Linwood Holton
Executive Board Chairman

Dean Burch
William T. Coleman, Jr.
William Frenzel
Richard G. Hatcher
Austin Ranney
Robert S. Strauss
Anne Wexler

GOVERNORS

Professor Herbert Alexander
Alan Baron
The Hon. Andrew Biemiller
Nolan Bushnell
The Hon. Tony Coelho
The Hon. William S. Cohen
Thomas E. Cronin
Lloyd N. Cutler
The Hon. Mendel J. Davis
Morris Dees
The Hon. Dave Durenberger
Julius Duscha
The Hon. Wendell H. Ford
The Hon. John H. Glenn, Jr.
The Hon. Edith Green
The Hon. Chuck Hardwick
Joseph Harrison
Richard Headlee
Stephen Hess
David A. Keene
The Hon. Martha Keys

Richard Richards
Carroll Kilpatrick
The Hon. Mary A. Marshall
The Hon. Eugene McCarthy
The Hon. George McGovern
Reg Murphy
Ms. Eleanor Holmes Norton
The Hon. Robert Packwood
The Hon. Thomas E. Petri
Jane Cahill Pfeiffer
The Hon. Albert H. Quie
The Hon. Tom Railsback
Richard Scammon
Ray Scherer
Stanley K. Sheinbaum
Mrs. Paula Unruh
Sander Vanocur
Robert P. Visser

ex officio
Charles T. Manatt

*The Executive Board of the Commission on the Presidential Nominating Process accepts full responsibility for the content of this Report. While the Governors have given advice and made proposals, to which the Board has given the fullest consideration, the members of the Board are the sole authors of the Report.